Building
CONTENT
LITERACY

Building
CONTENT LITERACY

Strategies for the Adolescent Learner

ROBERTA L. SEJNOST
SHARON M. THIESE

CORWIN
A SAGE Company

For information:

Corwin
A SAGE Company
2455 Teller Road
Thousand Oaks, California 91320
(800) 233-9936
Fax: (800) 417-2466
www.corwin.com

SAGE Ltd.
1 Oliver's Yard
55 City Road
London EC1Y 1SP
United Kingdom

SAGE India Pvt. Ltd.
B 1/I 1 Mohan Cooperative
   Industrial Area
Mathura Road, New Delhi 110 044
India

SAGE Asia-Pacific Pte. Ltd.
33 Pekin Street #02-01
Far East Square
Singapore 048763

Printed in the United States of America.

Library of Congress Cataloging-in-Publication Data

Sejnost, Roberta.
Building content literacy : strategies for the adolescent learner/Roberta L. Sejnost and Sharon M. Thiese.
    p. cm.
Includes bibliographical references and index.
ISBN 978-1-4129-5715-1 (pbk.)

   1. Language arts (Secondary) 2. Language arts—Correlation with content subjects.
I. Thiese, Sharon. II. Title.

LB1631.S457 2010
428.0071'2—dc22   2009038909

This book is printed on acid-free paper.

14   15   16   17   18   10   9   8   7   6   5   4   3   2

Acquisitions Editor:	Cathy Hernandez
Editorial Assistant:	Sarah Bartlett
Production Editor:	Cassandra Margaret Seibel
Copy Editor:	Cate Huisman
Typesetter:	C&M Digitals (P) Ltd.
Proofreader:	Susan Schon
Indexer:	Wendy Allex
Cover Designer:	Michael Dubowe

Contents

Preface

Research tells us the most effective teachers of content area literacy are the content area teachers themselves because, as content area specialists, they know what knowledge and skills are needed to effectively read and write in their disciplines. In effect, they think like scientists, artists, social scientists, mathematicians, or practitioners of whatever subject they teach. Yet, most middle school and high school teachers will readily admit that the majority of their training in college was in their content area discipline rather than in how to teach literacy in that discipline.

This book presents a snapshot of adolescent learners and how they learn, and it offers research-based best practices and content area strategies for teaching grounded in the theory of multiple intelligences and brain-based research. These enable teachers to increase student learning in all content area disciplines by more effectively integrating reading, writing, and critical thinking into their daily classroom instruction. Examples and reproducible masters for implementing the strategies are included in this book to assure immediate transfer to all content area classrooms.

Chapter 1 (The Challenge of Adolescent Literacy) highlights the challenge that teaching adolescents often presents; then it details ways in which teachers in today's classrooms can meet this challenge by presenting students with effective approaches to reading both narrative and expository texts.

Chapter 2 (Teaching Specialized and Technical Vocabulary) stresses the critical importance of helping students acquire, learn, and retain vocabulary by noting that the end product of both recreational and informational reading is comprehension and that vocabulary knowledge makes up as much as 70% to 80% of comprehension. To help facilitate the learning of vocabulary, this chapter provides a myriad of strategies to foster vocabulary acquisition and knowledge in all content areas.

Chapter 3 (Reading to Learn in Content Area Disciplines) discusses specific processes and skills that students must be able to complete in order to successfully comprehend both the narrative and expository texts they are required to read in the various content area disciplines they study. This chapter provides four types of learning strategies that can be used in all content area disciplines: (1) questioning strategies, (2) note-taking and summary strategies, (3) study guide strategies, and (4) critical response strategies.

Chapter 4 (Writing to Learn in Content Area Disciplines) examines the connection between reading and writing, noting that one must have access to written material for reading to occur. Furthermore, the act of writing enables students to process the ideas and concepts they have read about. In order to help students use writing to effectively learn what has been read, this chapter provides a variety of writing-to-learn strategies for use in all content area disciplines.

Chapter 5 (Speaking to Learn in Content Area Disciplines) examines the connection between reading and speaking, noting that during speaking, students not only process the ideas and concepts of their learning but also give concrete shape to their thoughts. In order to help students use speaking to effectively learn what has been read, this chapter provides a variety of speaking-to-learn strategies for use in all content area disciplines.

Chapter 6 (Fostering Real World Literacy) considers the challenges that face students in the age of technology and discusses the new literacies that engage students, such as the Internet, informational literacy, media literacy, and visual literacy. In order to help students learn using these new technological opportunities, this chapter provides learning strategies that can be used in all content areas for information-gathering and analysis activities, such as the following: (1) collaborative projects; (2) problem-based project learning; (3) media literacy, with activities for learning from newspapers, magazines, and news broadcasts; and finally (4) visual literacy, with activities that use storyboards, photographs, television, and videos.

Acknowledgments

We wish to thank Sheryl Sejnost and Sheila Ruh for their help and advice on digital literacy.

PUBLISHER'S ACKNOWLEDGMENTS

Corwin gratefully acknowledges the contributions of the following reviewers:

Wendy Caszatt-Allen, Eighth Grade
   Language Arts Teacher
Mid-Prairie Middle School
Kalona, IA

Susan Chase-Foster, Seventh Grade
   Language Arts Teacher
Fairhaven Middle School
Bellingham, WA

Johneen Griffin
Director of Secondary Pupil Services
Olentangy Local Schools
Lewis Center, OH

Janice Hall, Associate Professor of
   Secondary Education—Retired
Utah State University
Logan, UT

Timothy U. Kaufman
Associate Professor
University of Wisconsin, Green Bay
Green Bay, WI

Roxanne Farwick Owens
Chair, Teacher Education,
   DePaul University
Chicago, IL

Rusti Russow
Director of Teaching and Learning
Kankakee School District
Kankakee, IL

Nancy W. Sindelar
Educational Consultant
Chicago, IL

Nancy V. Workman
Professor of English
Lewis University
Romeoville, IL

About the Authors

Roberta L. Sejnost received her bachelor of arts from Elmhurst College, her master of education from the University of Illinois at Chicago, and her doctorate of education in curriculum and instruction from Loyola University, Chicago. She is currently a university professor at Loyola University, Chicago, and a literacy and assessment consultant to the Regional Office of Education, Kane County, Illinois. Sejnost has taught social studies, reading, and English at the secondary school level and courses in literacy, authentic assessment, brain-based learning, multiple intelligences, and cooperative learning at the college level. She is currently the International Reading Association's state coordinator for Illinois, and she has been a member of the board of directors for the International Reading Association's Secondary Reading Special Interest Group as well as a member of the executive board of the Illinois Reading Council and officer in several of the Illinois Reading Council's special interest groups.

A nationally recognized staff developer, Sejnost is a certified trainer in authentic assessment, brain-based learning, portfolio assessment, multiple intelligences, and reading and writing across content areas. She has presented at more than 200 educational conferences across the country. In addition to coauthoring this text, Sejnost was featured in the videotapes to accompany Drake University's online course EDDL 219—Reading Across the Curriculum. In 1986, she was named teacher of the year in her district; in 1993, she was awarded the International Reading Association's Contribution to Literacy Award for the State of Illinois; in 1996, she was recognized in *Who's Who of American Educators;* in 2003, she was given the Reading Educator of the Year award by the Illinois Reading Council; and in 2007 she was awarded a Certificate of Recognition by the Illinois Reading Council for her contributions to literacy in Illinois.

Sharon M. Thiese received a master of arts in English from Northeastern University and a master of arts in writing from National-Louis University, Chicago. She is also certified in gifted education and a member of Illinois Association for Gifted Children. In addition, Sharon is a certified trainer in gifted education, authentic assessment, multiple intelligences, portfolios, differentiation, and reading and writing across content areas, and she has presented at numerous local and statewide workshops and conferences. Thiese currently teaches writing at Lewis University, Romeoville, Illinois, and graduate classes for Aurora University, Aurora, Illinois. She taught English and writing at Geneva High School in Geneva, Illinois, and has been Geneva Community Unit 304's high school educator of the year. She is also recognized in *Who's Who of American Educators.*

The Challenge of Adolescent Literacy

Adolescence is the conjugator of childhood and adulthood.

Louise J. Kaplan

WHAT IS THE CHALLENGE?

No one, we believe, will argue with the fact that teaching adolescents today is a challenge. A walk through the halls of a typical high school of today provides an eye-opening exploration into the world of adolescent literacy in the 21st century.

Elliot transferred from a large urban district in the city. He likes drafting class, but does not do well in other classes and feels school has little to offer him. He does not read well, is far behind in academic credits, and is often introverted and depressed. Most of his grades are Ds and Fs.

Molly loves the fun parts of school, most of her teachers, and all of her friends. The social part of school is what she lives for. She is a C student.

Gabe lives in a foster home and has just returned to regular school from an alternative program. He is often truant and rarely bothers with class assignments or homework. He earns Fs in all his classes.

Theresa is the ideal student. She works hard, faithfully completes all her assignments, and often requests extra credit assignments. She earns As and Bs.

Depal is the only girl in her family. She, her brothers, and her parents came from Pakistan two years ago, where her brothers went to school regularly; she did not. In America, she goes to school, but she is often absent, because she must stay home and watch her younger brothers when they are ill. Her parents cannot afford the luxury of missing a day of work. Depal has an ELL resource class, where she earns Bs; she is not passing any of her academic classes. Her greatest challenge is reading the assignments her teachers give.

Juan Carlos has just recently arrived from the foothills of the Sierra Madre Mountains. He never attended school before, and the requirement that he meet the school bus on time often prevents him from coming to school now. He is in an ELL resource class where he receives Cs; in academic classes he receives Fs; he readily admits he cannot understand or read English very well.

Perhaps teaching adolescents has always been a challenge; as far back as 1984, Ted Sizer had these words to offer:

> Besides their age, they have in common the vulnerability that comes with inexperience and a social status bordering on limbo. They are children, but they are adults, too. Many are ready and able to work, but are dissuaded from doing so. They can bear children, but are counseled not to. They can kill, and sometimes they do. They can act autonomously but are told what to do. . . . They share the pain of a stereotype, of gum-chewing, noisy, careless, blooming sexual creatures who are allowed to have fun but not too much of it. (Sizer, 1984, p. 33)

No matter what challenge these young people might offer up, there are those of us who want and need to teach them, and they need to learn. However, their learning, according to national test results, is also a challenge, and some might even say it is in a state of crisis. Since 1969, the National Assessment of Educational Progress (NAEP) has measured the educational progress of our students by administering subject-area assessments to students aged 9, 13, and 17. The NAEP reading assessment measures the reading comprehension of students by assessing their ability to

1. carry out simple discrete reading tasks (Level 150), such as following brief written directions; selecting words, phrases, and sentences to describe a simple picture; and interpreting simple written clues to identify a common object. At this level, they have difficulty making inferences.

2. demonstrate partially developed skills and understanding (Level 200), such as locating and identifying facts from simple informational paragraphs, stories, and articles. At this level, they can combine ideas and make inferences based on short, uncomplicated passages.

3. interrelate ideas and make generalizations (Level 250), such as using intermediate skills and strategies to search for, locate, and organize the information they find in relatively lengthy passages and can recognize what these passages have paraphrased. At this level, students can make generalizations and inferences about the main idea and the author's purpose in passages of literature, science, and social studies.

4. understand complicated information (Level 300), such as complicated literary and informational passages, including content area materials. At this level, they can analyze and integrate less familiar content area material and can provide reactions to and explanations of text as a whole.

5. learn from specialized reading materials (Level 350). At this level, they can extend and restructure the ideas they read in specialized and complex texts like scientific materials, literary essays, and historical documents. They are also able to understand the links between ideas, even if these links are not explicitly stated. Finally, they are able to make appropriate generalizations. (NAEP, 2005a)

The NAEP numeric levels described above are defined by the following terms:

- Below Basic: Students have achieved less than partial mastery.
- Basic: Students have achieved partial mastery of prerequisite knowledge and skills that are fundamental for proficient work at each grade. (To be considered to have achieved this level of mastery, students must score at least 243 in Grade 8 and 265 in Grade 12.)
- Proficient: Students have shown solid academic performance for each grade assessed. Students who reach this level have demonstrated competency over challenging subject matter, including knowledge, application of that knowledge to real world situations, and analytical skills appropriate to the subject matter. (To be considered to have achieved this level of mastery, students must score at least 281 in Grade 8 and 302 in Grade 12.)
- Advanced: Students have demonstrated superior performance. (To be considered to have achieved this level of mastery, students must score at least 323 in Grade 8 and 346 in Grade 12.) (NAEP, 2005b)

The NAEP was administered to eighth graders in 2007 and to twelfth graders in 2005. In looking at the trends of student performance, we can understand the concern many have regarding a crisis in adolescent literacy.

- Both male and female students' scores declined in comparison to scores from students who were in the same grades in 1992.

- While the percentage of eighth-grade students performing at or above the Basic level increased, there was no significant change in the percentage of eighth-grade students scoring at or above the Proficient level.

- The percentage of twelfth-grade students performing at or above the Basic level decreased from 80% in 1992 to 73% in 2005, while the percentage of twelfth-grade students performing at or above the Proficient level decreased from 40% to 35%.

- In sum, when the scores of 2005 and 2007 are compared to the scores of 1992, a decline is seen across all performance levels except in the scores of students performing at the 90th percentile. That is, the scores of the top 10% of students were just as high in 2005 and 2007 as they had been in 1992. For the other 90% of students, scores dropped during that period. (NAEP, 2005b)

And the challenge of adolescent literacy crosses all boundaries as well. Further examination of the NAEP trend data shows the following:

- The score gaps between White and Black students and White and Hispanic students have remained constant since 1992.

- At the eighth-grade level, Blacks scored, on average, 27 points lower on the reading assessment than Whites, and Hispanics scored, on average, 25 points lower than Whites.

- At the twelfth-grade level, White and Black students were the only racial/ethnic groups to show a statistically significant difference in reading performance, scoring lower in 2005 than twelfth graders scored in 1992.

- The performance gap between the genders has widened, with female students continually outscoring male students since 1971. Twelfth-grade females outscored males by 13 points in 1992, and at the eighth-grade level, female students scored 10 points higher than male students. Such gender score gaps are not significantly different from the gaps seen 15 years ago. (Lee, Grigg, & Donahue, 2007)

The above data clearly illustrate that the adolescents of today may possess basic literacy but may not possess the advanced skills they need to successfully function in the world of tomorrow. And, the report *Reading Next—A Vision for Action and Research in Middle and High School Literacy* (Biancarosa & Snow, 2004) supports this conjecture with some very alarming statistics:

- Eight million students in Grades 4–12 have been identified as struggling readers.

- More than 3,000 students drop out of high school every day.

- Only 70% of today's high school students graduate with a regular diploma in the usual four-year time frame.
- During their postsecondary educational experience, 53% of high school graduates enroll in remedial courses.

Biancarosa and Snow lay the blame for this crisis on that fact that adolescents today "can *read* words accurately, but they do not *comprehend* what they read" (p. 8) and conclude with the statement that today's adolescents "lack the strategies to help them comprehend what they read" (p. 8).

HOW CAN WE MEET THE CHALLENGE?

Thus, if today's adolescents are, indeed, in a literacy crisis, what can we, as educators, do to help? Glenda Beamon Crawford (2007) suggests that a possible reason for the widening gap in adolescent literacy is "the growing 'disconnect' between adolescents' lives and school experiences" (p. 41) and notes that "adolescent learning involves interactive, purposeful, and meaningful engagement" (p. 5); it happens best when adolescents

- encounter developmentally appropriate learning that is presented in multiple ways and in interesting and enjoyable manners.
- are intellectually challenged by authentic tasks that they perceive to be challenging, novel, and relevant to their lives.
- share and discuss ideas and work collaboratively on tasks, projects, and problems.
- utilize multiple strategies to acquire, integrate, and interpret knowledge meaningfully and then demonstrate their understanding and apply their recently found knowledge to new situations.
- are provided opportunities to develop and use strategic thinking skills to reason and problem solve.
- are given guidance and immediate feedback on their progress and encouraged to monitor and reflect upon their personal progress and understanding.
- are situated in a safe, supportive environment where their personal ideas are valued, and they are free from fear of punishment and embarrassment. (Crawford, 2007)

In addition, as teachers, we know that learning occurs when students are motivated, and Crawford (2007) suggests that adolescents are motivated when they (1) study a curriculum that intrigues them and stimulates their curiosity, (2) can express their personal and creative ideas, (3) work collegially with peers and others, and (4) are able to see their work is of high quality and valuable to those around them. Guthrie and Davis (2003) and Reeves (2004) have conducted research in which they have invited adolescents themselves to offer some thoughts into what motivates them. While some adolescents admit that the difficulty of the texts they are asked to read is a barrier to their reading, most of the adolescents surveyed report that their lack of interest in what they are given to read is a greater barrier (Lenters, 2006). In addition, Ivey (1999) reports that adolescents are motivated to read if they have an authentic purpose for doing so.

CONTENT AREA LITERACY

Understanding how adolescents learn best does not solve all the problems embedded in the adolescent literacy crisis that exists. Reading is a different task when we read literature than it is when we read science texts, historical analyses, newspapers, or tax forms. This is why teaching students how to read the texts of different academic disciplines is a key part of teaching these disciplines (WestEd, 2002). As students move through school, they usually become quite comfortable with the elements of narrative or story reading. Even the authors' primary school grandchildren can identify the elements of narrative reading, such as main character, setting, and plot. However, as students enroll in middle and high school, they are faced with new reading demands. Suddenly they are required to read and comprehend texts that are difficult and are of an informational rather than narrative nature. These texts are factual and often organized around abstract concepts presented as a hierarchy of main ideas and supporting details. In addition, these informational texts contain longer text segments and content-specific vocabulary. In effect, middle and high school students must become content literate. Content literacy, as defined by Vacca and Vacca (2008) is "the ability to use reading, writing, talking, listening, and viewing to learn subject matter in a given discipline" (p. 10).

To be content literate, adolescents must be able to locate information and understand it; they must be able to compare and evaluate the variety of sources of information they have located, and they must be able to successfully interpret, generalize, synthesize, and apply the information gleaned from these sources (Roe, Stoodt-Hill, & Burns, 2007). Today's adolescents read and write for a variety of purposes; among them are to learn, do, locate information, solve problems, follow directions, perform job functions, and carry out everyday functions as well as for fun. In effect, content literate adolescents must acquire and apply reading and writing strategies to construct knowledge rather than just gain information. And, these thoughts clearly align with the recommendations for effective content area instruction made by Biancarosa and Snow in their *Reading Next* (2004) report. The report recommends that all students receive explicit instruction in reading comprehension and intensive writing in all content area classes, advocates that students be taught not only to read from texts but to learn from them, and emphasizes the need for greater student engagement and motivation and for more opportunities for students to work collaboratively with each other as they study texts. Both the report of the National Reading Panel (National Reading Panel, 2000) and the RAND report on reading comprehension (RAND Reading Study Group, 2002), along with Santa (2006), posit that effective content area instruction includes the following:

- Integrating strategy instruction into content area learning by teaching students to utilize a repertoire of comprehension strategies, such as question generation, question-answer routines, comprehension monitoring, cooperative learning, summarizing, and graphic organizers when they read challenging text
- Focusing on discipline-specific vocabulary knowledge
- Exposing students to various types of genres, such as expository and narrative texts
- Providing student choice in assignments, challenging tasks, and opportunities for collaborative work with their peers

Thus, in order to become content literate, students need general literacy skills like activating prior knowledge, interpreting facts accurately, identifying main ideas and supporting details, drawing conclusions and making inferences, and monitoring and repairing their comprehension. But they also need to make use of content-specific literacy skills. And, these skills differ from one content area discipline to another. Furthermore, content reading instruction is most effective when teachers guide student learning as they teach them their content area disciplines (Biancarosa & Snow, 2004; National Reading Panel, 2000; RAND Reading Study Group, 2002). A complete discussion of the skills necessary for successful learning in each content area discipline as well as strategies to scaffold student learning of these disciplines will be discussed below in the section on reading informational text.

MEETING THE STANDARDS

In addition to helping the adolescent become content literate, the road to developing adolescents into effective readers and learners must also include attention to the learning standards that govern what has been deemed important for students to know and be able to do at each stage of their learning journey. Today all states as well as several national and education organizations have created educational standards or guidelines. These national organizations include the following: the National Council of Teachers of Mathematics, National Council of Teachers of English, National Council for the Social Studies, National Council on Economic Education, Center for Civic Education, Consortium of National Arts Education Associations, International Society for Technology in Education, and National Academies of Science.

Standards describe what students are expected to know, understand, and be able to do at each grade level. Schools design a curriculum to help students meet these standards. Three kinds of educational standards are used in schools today: content standards, performance standards, and opportunity-to-learn standards.

• Content standards establish what skills and knowledge students should be able to learn by the end of a unit and why they need to learn them. Since effective instruction requires a purposeful and meaningful approach to teaching the content, teachers need to consider which strategies will promote learning the skills and content and to determine which standard(s) the students can master.

• Performance standards describe different levels of attainment and mastery. These standards are like rubrics, because they depict how well students meet the content standards. A performance standard has levels (4, 3, 2, and 1; or advanced, proficient, novice, and basic). The meaning of each score is explained, and frequently examples of student work are provided for each level.

• Opportunity-to-learn or school standards detail the resources schools have in order to be able to meet the standards. Educators believed that schools need to have the necessary staff, programs, and supplies to meet government standards.

Adhering to the Standards

Although the establishment of national standards does not guarantee success for all schools, the standards do provide clear expectations to improve teacher instruction and to raise the academic achievement of all children. They also supply information to administrators, employers, schools, parents, and students that explains how their school's achievement compares with that of other schools.

Standards should guide the way teachers plan lessons and activities in the core subjects: mathematics, science, language arts, and social studies. Teachers need to set clear expectations for all students with every lesson they teach; they need to design tasks that help students attain the standards and to create scoring guides to let students know how they can meet the standards. Meeting all of these expectations can be a difficult task. Grant Wiggins and Jay McTighe (2005) advocate the idea of backward design, or considering what the standards require and then mapping backwards to identify the core learning situations and assessments that will reinforce the attainment of the standards.

THE CHALLENGE OF READING DIVERSE TEXTS

The advent of a standards-based curriculum designed to raise achievement leads, naturally, to a realization of the impact reading comprehension has on that achievement, especially at the middle and high school level, when reading demands increase. Woodward and Elliott (1990) note that between 67% and 90%

of classroom instruction at the secondary level involves textbooks as the prime focus. Thus, as students move from elementary to secondary school, they are often required to read great amounts of text independently. However, as Vacca and Vacca (2008) state, "A gap often exists between the ideas and relationships they are studying and their prior knowledge, interests, attitudes, cultural background, language proficiency, or reading ability" (p. 39). And, to add to the burden, according to Allington (2002) and Budiansky (2001), many of the texts students are required to read are written two or more years above their grade level.

In what ways, then, can we, as teachers, help alleviate this possible mismatch between students' reading ability and the text they must read? One way that has been proven effective is the use of instructional scaffolding, a method by which teachers support students' efforts to read and understand their texts. Instructional scaffolds, much like the scaffolds used in building construction, provide students with the support needed to attempt new tasks by supplying them with specific and effective strategies for completing these tasks.

One of the prime areas in which teachers can scaffold their students' learning is in differentiating between reading narrative texts and reading informational or expository texts. These two kinds of texts require very different reading skills, and teachers must be aware of the text characteristics and the specific skills students need to read these two kinds of texts in order to help them learn effectively. The following section will discuss the specific demands each text type presents as well as some scaffolding strategies to help students meet these diverse demands with competence.

READING NARRATIVE TEXT

Narrative text includes any type of writing that relates a series of events and includes both fiction (novels, short stories, poems) and nonfiction (memoirs, biographies, news stories). Both forms tell stories that use imaginative language and express emotion, often through the use of imagery, metaphors, and symbols. Students need to know how narrative texts work and how to read them, because stories are used for many important purposes. The purpose of narrative text is to entertain, to gain and hold a reader's interest; however, writers of memoirs and novels often relate complex stories that examine universal ideas, events, and issues. In addition, speakers, advertisers, and politicians use stories to persuade us to accept or reject an idea.

In effect, students need to learn the purposes and methods of narration in order to understand the narrative framework and to eliminate frustration when they read. When students know the narrative elements, they can more easily follow the story line and make successful predictions about what is to occur. In addition, understanding these elements develops higher-level thinking skills. For example, the complications in a plot are related to cause and effect, and awareness of character's motives can lead to analysis.

All in all, the narrative form is unique, because authors relate ideas they want to express about how people behave and what they believe. These ideas, or themes, generally relate to universal truths and make connections to the reader's experiences.

Scaffolding Strategies for Narrative Text

Teachers can use the following techniques to introduce the narrative form.

Focus Strategy

1. Focus: Themes
   a. Ask students to do prewriting about a theme. Examples: List four of your fears; be ready to discuss one. Write about a time you experienced fear.
   b. Ask small groups to make posters related to a theme or themes. Example: Students can define a theme, identify positive and negative examples, create a symbol, and write a one-sentence assertion about the theme.

2. Focus: Conflict
   a. Ask students to identify modern values and record their answers.
   b. Have the class identify the values that are evident in the narrative.
   c. In small groups, have students determine how the characters' values cause conflict.
   d. Create a series of questions, each starting with the word *suppose,* that relate to a character's conflicts and complications. Example: Suppose you were not allowed to see the one you loved?

3. Focus: Features
   a. Ask students to copy lines from the narrative that relate to the conflict or characters; break the lines into three parts, and write each part on a different color index card. Mix the cards together, and then ask students to work together to find complete lines. Then have them read the line aloud and make a prediction. Example:

   Line 1: "That's true." She hesitated.

   Line 2: "Well, I've had a very bad time, Nick,"

   Line 3: "and I'm pretty cynical about everything." (p. 16, *The Great Gatsby*)

   b. Ask students to make predictions about the title and/or illustrations in the text. Example: What does the title, *A Separate Peace,* suggest?

4. Focus: Characterization

   Utilize the strategy AWAIT. To teach the methods of indirect characterization, have each student create an image of a character. Each image should include the following details:

Appearance: What does the character look like? Wear?

Words: Create a line of dialogue that the character would say.

Actions: Make the character do something (e.g., run, hit a ball).

Interactions with other characters: Write a sentence that creates a conflict between the character and someone else.

Thoughts: Create a thought bubble; record the character's thoughts in the bubble.

In addition, have each student write a one-line assertion stating what the character is like.

Students can easily remember indirect characterization by learning the acronym AWAIT.

5. Focus: Setting

Use the graphic organizer in Figure 1.1 to teach the functions of the setting. Ask students to create an example for each function.

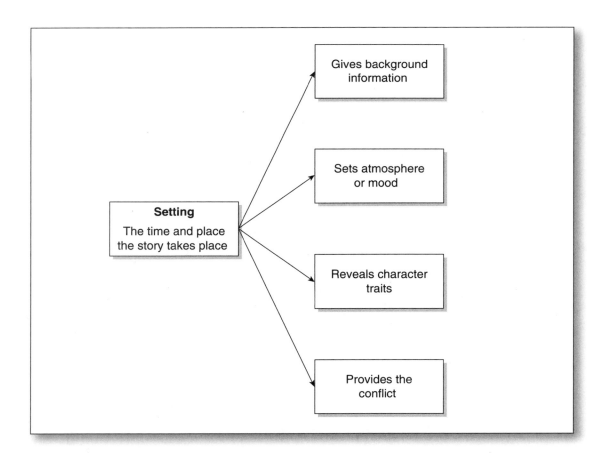

Figure 1.1 Function of Setting

READING EXPOSITORY TEXT

Expository text differs greatly from narrative text in tone, style, structure, and features. First, expository texts purvey a tone of authority, since the authors possess authentic and accurate information on the subjects they write about (Fisher & Frey, 2008). Second, these texts follow a style that is distinctly different from that of narrative text. Expository text uses clear, focused language and moves from facts that are general to specific and abstract to concrete. In addition, Fisher and Frey suggest that texts in each content area discipline exhibit specific styles. These specific styles will be discussed in Chapter 3 of this text.

Another aspect of expository texts is that they utilize specific structures to present and explain information (Burke, 2000). And, it has long been known that the ability to recognize text structure enhances the student's ability to comprehend and recall the information read (Armbruster, Anderson, & Ostertag, 1989; McGee, 1982; Meyer & Poon, 2001; Niles, 1974; Taylor & Samuels, 1983). The five most common structures utilized in informational text are cause-effect, comparison-contrast, definition-example, problem-solution, and proposition-support or sequential listing. To help students recognize and identify these structures, teachers can acquaint them with the signal or cue words authors utilize in writing each of the structures (See Figure 1.2). In addition, Doug Buehl (2001) has created a series of questions to help guide students in identifying each specific structure. Finally, Figure 1.3 is a reproducible master

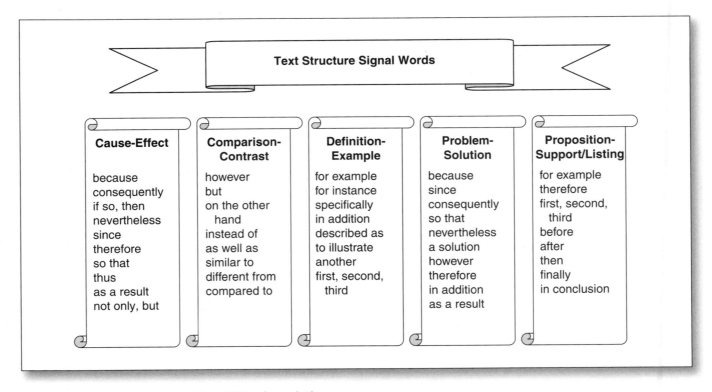

Figure 1.2 Text Structure Signal Words and Phrases

TEXT STRUCTURE ORGANIZERS

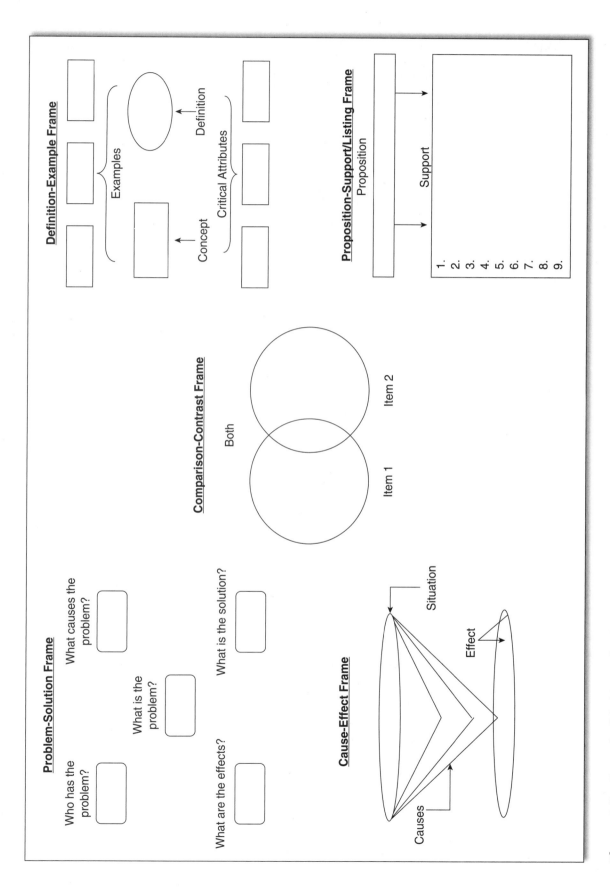

Figure 1.3   Reproducible Master for Text Structure Organizers

for a set of graphic organizers that students and teachers may use to facilitate structure identification.

A final aspect of informational text is its features or those items that an author uses to organize the text. Common text features include the following: (1) a table of contents, (2) a preface, (3) chapter introductions, (4) chapter headings and subheadings, (5) marginal notes or gloss, (6) chapter summaries, (7) maps, charts, graphs, and illustrations, (8) an index, and (9) a glossary. As noted above, content reading instruction is most effective when teachers scaffold their students' learning (Biancarosa & Snow, 2004; National Reading Panel, 2000; Rhoder, 2002). While presenting a structural overview as a scaffolding strategy is a good place to begin, Garber-Miller (2007) advises, "It is also beneficial to give students a content overview so they can ponder the many concepts and questions they will encounter throughout the year. Teachers must help them understand how the ideas in the textbook are interrelated" (p. 285). She suggests that teachers utilize text previews in order to accomplish this. Several textbook previews are presented below.

Scaffolding Strategies for Expository Text

Text Structure Strategy

Readence, Bean, and Baldwin (2004) suggest a simple procedure to help students recognize, identify, and utilize text structure as a way to better comprehend and recall reading from expository text:

Steps to Recognize Expository Text Structure

1. First, model this strategy for students by working through an assigned text reading that illustrates a particular text structure and explaining why it is a certain type and how that type is organized. Make use of the text structure signal words provided in Figure 1.2, and use the graphic organizer from among those in Figure 1.3 that is illustrative of the type of text being explained.

2. Next, provide students with a practice session so they can utilize the signal words and graphic organizers for each text structure pattern. This second step allows you to gradually shift the responsibility of learning about text structures from yourself to the students.

3. Finally, when students have become proficient at identifying specific text structure patterns, they should produce examples of the various structures on their own.

In order to further reinforce students' understanding of text structure, you can utilize the Structured Notetaking procedure (Smith & Tompkins, 1988) to develop study guides based on the text structure of assigned readings.

Steps for Structured Notetaking

1. Select a section of text and determine the organizational pattern used to convey information in the text. Common organizational patterns and questions that can be used to guide student reading are discussed above.

2. Next, create a graphic organizer that follows this pattern, complete with focusing questions, and distribute it as a study guide. (See the reproducible master in Figure 1.3 and an example for science in Figure 1.4.)

3. Instruct students to read the chapter and take notes by recording the appropriate information in the graphic organizer sections.

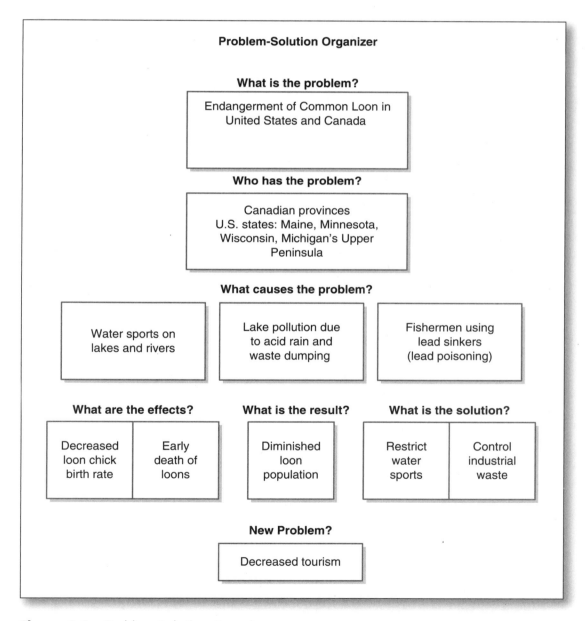

Figure 1.4   Problem-Solution Organizer

Text Previews

The driving force in most content area classes is the textbook. As noted earlier, Woodward and Elliott (1990) tell us that often 67% to 90% of secondary school classroom instruction is centered around the text, making it the prime provider of content information. Also as noted earlier, we are well aware that the reading difficulty of the texts used in secondary school classrooms often far exceed the reading abilities of the students who use them (Allington, 2002; Budiansky, 2001). And to make the situation even more complex, the students that inhabit our classrooms are often reluctant readers and thus unwilling to read their texts at all. However, given the importance placed upon textbooks by content area teachers, we cannot allow students to merely ignore the reading tasks required of them.

What can we do, then, to help our students as they face the tremendous task of achieving content area literacy? Karen Garber-Miller (2007) suggests that one way teachers can "scaffold their students to reading success" (p. 285) is to provide students with textbook previewing strategies that focus not only on the structure of the text—such as the table of contents, index, chapter introductions, and so forth—but on a content overview, which focuses on the concepts and questions covered in the chapter and their interrelationships. Examples of some innovative text previews (Name that Feature, Textbook Sales Pitches/Commercials, and What's Old? What's New?), as well as general steps for previewing text, as developed by Garber-Miller (2007) are detailed below. It is imperative, however, that teachers model the preview strategy they will utilize first, so students clearly understand the process.

General Steps for a Text Preview

1. Instruct students to peruse the text, searching for important or recurrent features. (It is especially crucial that the teacher model this step first, before asking students to complete it.)

2. Group students into teams, and ask them to choose a recorder to record their findings.

3. Have each student share his or her findings with the group.

4. Ask students to report their group findings to the entire class. (At this point, if you notice students have overlooked an important feature, inform them to add it to the list.)

5. Once all groups have reported out, assign each group a feature or features, and ask them to generate a written description of what each feature does for the book. Collect these descriptions.

Variations of Text Previews

Name That Feature

If you have several classes completing the feature descriptions described above, you can utilize the descriptions to play "Name That Feature":

1. Assemble the class into teams; have each team elect a spokesperson.

2. Read each description developed by another class aloud, and challenge the teams to identify the feature.

3. Allow student teams time to discuss their response and, when a team has an answer, the team spokesperson should stand. The first one to stand should attempt the answer. (You may, of course, also provide a bell or a buzzer to signal that an answer is known.)

4. Award one point per correct answer; the team with the most points at the game's conclusion wins.

Textbook Sales Pitch/Commercials

1. Divide the class into two groups and distribute textbooks to each group.

2. Members of Group 1 assume the role of a textbook salesperson. Allow preparation time for the group to peruse the text to get an understanding of its organization, special features, benefits, and weaknesses. Inform them that their task is to prepare a persuasive sales pitch for the textbook to an audience of skeptical teachers.

3. Members of Group 2 assume the role of teachers and students who are serving on a textbook selection committee and are skeptical about choosing a new text. Allow preparation time for the group to peruse the text to compile a list of what they feel are important features in a textbook of good quality as well as a list of questions and concerns they will pose to the textbook salesperson based on their own review of the text.

4. When the presentation and discussion are complete, be sure to add any additional considerations you feel students have overlooked.

What's Old? What's New?

1. Divide students into small groups, and assign each group a text chapter to review.

2. Ask students to peruse the topics and special features they find within their chapter.

3. Have each group compile a list of primary topics the chapter covers and list them on a chart under either the heading *What's Old?* for content that has been covered in past classes or *What's New?* for material that is new or unfamiliar. (Note: Garber-Miller warns that due to varying past experiences, group members may disagree on whether topics are old or new; encourage them to reach consensus.) In addition, she stresses that it is especially crucial that the teacher model this step first before asking students to complete it.

4. Ask each group to display their charts and lead their classmates on a "chapter walk," pointing out the old and new concepts in each chapter. Encourage each group to seek feedback on their list.

SCAFFOLDING INSTRUCTION FOR SPECIAL NEEDS STUDENTS

The strategies included in this book have been used with students at all levels of achievement: students enrolled in honors classes, regular classes, and low-achieving classes as well as students who have been labeled remedial readers, students in special education classes, and English-language learners. The strategies have been used successfully when adapted by the teacher to meet the unique needs of each specific learner. However, it should be noted that certain practices and adaptations have been identified as being effective when working with special needs students, and these should be utilized when presenting the strategies detailed in this text.

First, as teachers, we recognize that students learn more when

1. they are actively engaged in their learning.

2. information is presented in small "chunks" rather than in large quantities.

3. abstract, complex concepts are presented in concrete ways.

4. information is presented in an organized fashion.

5. students make connections between new information learned and their previous knowledge.

6. graphic organizers are used.

7. students follow a set of procedures or steps.

8. teachers give directions orally, and in writing, and by demonstrating or modeling what is expected.

All of the strategies presented in this text incorporate these elements.

Second, as Deschenes, Ebeling, and Sprague (1994) note, sometimes teachers must allow students to use alternate instructional materials or make changes in the learning environment. They offer nine ways in which this may be done. Teachers may adapt instruction according to the

1. **size** of the assignment, by adapting the number of items or facts a student is expected to learn or to complete, such as reducing the number of vocabulary terms required.

2. **time** for the assignment, by adapting the time allotted for a student to learn a concept or complete a task.

3. **input** provided, by adapting the way they deliver the strategy to a student, such as using visual aids, concrete examples, hands-on activities, or cooperative learning.

4. **output** to be provided, by adapting how a student is asked to exhibit what he or she has learned, such as responding in verbal and tactile ways as well as written ones.

5. **difficulty** of the assignment, by adapting the skill level, problem type, or parameters of how a student may complete the tasks assigned, such as by simplifying task instructions or allowing a student to use a calculator, a computer, or something comparable.

6. **degree of participation** required, by adapting the extent to which a student is involved in the task, such as being the materials manager in a cooperative group rather than the reporter.

7. **level of support** provided, by adapting the amount of scaffolding or support a student is given, such as assigning a partner, an instructional aide, or a tutor to help a student complete the assigned task.

8. **goals** of the assignment, by adapting the outcomes that a student is expected to achieve, such as asking some students to learn the names of various whales while asking other students to compare one type of whale to another.

9. **curriculum,** by providing different instructional strategies or materials for a student, such as choosing a different piece of text or story for the student to read.

Again, all of the strategies in this text can be adapted in any of the nine ways listed above.

CHAPTER SUMMARY

Chapter 1 presents the challenge that teaching adolescents often presents and details ways teachers in today's classrooms can meet this challenge by presenting strategies students can use to effectively read narrative and expository texts. In addition, specific scaffolding strategies for both narrative and expository texts as well as suggestions on how to utilize the various strategies presented in this text with special needs students are presented.

CHAPTER 2

Teaching Specialized and Technical Vocabulary

The limits of my language are the limits of my mind.
All I know is what I have words for.

Ludwig Wittgenstein

THE IMPLICATION OF TEACHING VOCABULARY

The end product of recreational reading and reading other texts is comprehension. Comprehension and word recognition are highly related, and knowledge and use of vocabulary skills are effective predictors of comprehension ability. Nagy and Scott (2000) and Pressley (2002) tell us that vocabulary knowledge makes up as much as 70% to 80% of comprehension, so we cannot deny that vocabulary is of critical importance to comprehension. Furthermore, the positive correlation between vocabulary and comprehension is validated by the research of Beck, McKeown, and Kucan (2002) and Graves (2000). In addition, Allington (2006) and Samuels (2002) note that students with large vocabularies recognize more words and read more fluently than students with smaller vocabularies, and Stahl and Fairbanks (1986) tell us that students with large vocabularies understand text better and score higher on achievement tests than students with smaller vocabularies. In contrast, Vacca and Vacca (2008) remind us that students who do not know the meaning of a term guess the meaning, skip the passage, or stop reading altogether! Therefore, in order to help students succeed, teachers must help them make the connection between vocabulary and comprehension.

While teachers may recognize the importance of teaching vocabulary, recent research reveals that relatively little academic vocabulary instruction actually takes place. Durkin (1979) discovered that at the upper-elementary level, teachers spend less than 1% of their reading instruction time teaching vocabulary, and Nagy and Scott (2000) and Biemiller (2004) report that in the upper-elementary classrooms they observed, only 6% of total school time was devoted to vocabulary instruction, with only 1.4% allotted to content area vocabulary. Obviously, then, not enough instructional time in classrooms today is being devoted to vocabulary instruction. In addition, research also tells us that what we are doing to teach vocabulary may not be very effective! Greenwood (2004) declares, "There is a great divide between what we know about vocabulary and what we do" (p. 28).

This declaration is validated by both Nagy (1988) and Basurto (2004), who note that traditional vocabulary instruction for most teachers is simply having students look up words in the glossary or dictionary, write the definitions, memorize them, and use the words in a sentence, a practice Nagy calls "definition only." Irvin (1990) and Ryder and Graves (1994) criticize this prescriptive approach as being only minimally effective and resulting not only in student disengagement but in little student understanding of the text and only temporary retention of material. Furthermore, according to Scott and Nagy (1997) and Marzano (2004), most students struggle when they attempt to derive meaning from dictionary definitions. And it is easy to understand why. Most dictionary definitions are precise and concise, and they are seldom written in student friendly or age appropriate language, thus making it almost impossible for the student to determine an accurate definition. Furthermore, in our experience, when students are sent to locate a dictionary definition, they usually choose either the first definition that appears or the shortest definition that appears; neither of these choices, however, may be the correct choice! This is especially true in the case of content area vocabulary, which is often so specialized and technical that the definition is usually neither the first nor the shortest.

Another traditional vocabulary strategy teachers often utilize is asking students to decipher a word's meaning by its context. But, this, too, is an ineffective practice. Asking students to depend upon the surrounding context to determine a correct definition often fails the student as well. Beck et al. (2002) and Nagy, Herman, and Anderson (1985) note that the odds of a student deriving the intended meaning of a word utilizing its written context is very low, only 5% to 15%, since most contexts are often uninformative, because a single context rarely provides students with enough information to allow a productive inference to be made.

Since we have established that a problem exists with the way vocabulary is taught, what can be done to alleviate this problem? In other words, what constitutes effective vocabulary instruction? Blachowicz and Fisher (2002) have identified four main guidelines that characterize what effective vocabulary teachers should do. We would like to define these as "best practices for effective vocabulary instruction." Using these best practices, the effective vocabulary teacher

1. builds a word-rich environment in which students are immersed in words for both incidental and intentional learning.
2. helps students develop as independent word learners.
3. uses instructional strategies that not only teach vocabulary effectively but model good word-learning behaviors.
4. uses assessment that matches the goal of instruction.

Now, knowing what the best practices for effective vocabulary instruction are, how can we implement them in a classroom? In order to build a word-rich environment that facilitates both incidental and intentional word learning (Guideline 1 above), Blachowicz and Fisher (2002) suggest that first teachers need to be good models of word learning, thus showing students that word learning is a pleasurable experience. Second, according to Graves and Watts-Taffe (2002), teachers need to create a word-rich classroom that includes much reading (to children and by children); the availability of dictionaries, word puzzles, word calendars, and books of rhymes and riddles; and word-building activities such as A Word a Day or Mystery Word. To help students develop as independent word learners (Guideline 2 above), teachers must encourage their students to take control of their own learning. Nagy and Scott (2000) and Blachowicz and Fisher (2002) suggest that this is best accomplished by having students engage in the self-selection of words they both want and need to know. The third guideline, using instructional strategies that not only teach vocabulary effectively but model good word-learning behaviors, clarifies the importance of utilizing research-based strategies to help students learn new vocabulary words, and it can be accomplished by utilizing the strategies presented later in this chapter. Finally, the last guideline, using assessment that matches the goal of instruction, is best accomplished, according to Blachowicz and Fisher (2002), by making sure the assessments we give test both the depth and the breadth of the students' understanding of a word. For example, to test for the depth of knowledge students have, we want to know things such as whether they can recognize the meaning of a word in text and conversation, use the word appropriately, or define a word.

However, when we assess for the students' knowledge of the breadth of a word, we are interested in discovering whether they understand how words are connected to one another, such as whether they understand how viruses, bacteria, and illness are connected. We also want to know if they understand the levels of meaning a word has, such as whether they can differentiate between *old* as it refers to a condition as opposed to *old* as it refers to a stage of development.

TEACHING VOCABULARY IN CONTENT AREA DISCIPLINES

Even though we may utilize the best practices for effective vocabulary instruction, it is important to realize that teaching vocabulary in content area disciplines presents some unique problems. First, every discipline has its own technical, specialized vocabulary. These words are not used in everyday language but are employed regularly by specialists in a field. For example, biologists discuss the process of photosynthesis, while mathematicians discuss theorems. Because these terms are part of the discipline, students can have a better understanding of the discipline's concepts if they are familiar with the vocabulary terms that are applicable.

Second, content area vocabulary words are often technical in nature. And, because of that, common vocabulary words often assume a specialized meaning. Moreover, students are often very familiar with the common meaning of the word but fail to understand how that word might be used in a specific content discipline. Consider, for example, the definition a science teacher will require for the word *root*. Now consider how that definition will differ in a mathematics classroom, or in an English or language arts classroom or a social studies classroom. The variability of common words as they appear in specialized content disciplines was made clear in a lament an art teacher shared with Roberta. For almost a week the art teacher diligently taught the concept of *media* to her ninth grade Introduction to Art students. She carefully explained the techniques of watercolor, oil, pen and ink, chalk, and so forth to them. When it was time for an assessment, the art teacher asked students to provide three examples of media used in art. Can you guess how many of these ninth graders responded? Yes, their responses included the following: CDs, movies, text messaging, video games, television, Game Boy, X-Box, and Wii! These typical ninth graders, well versed in the media of the technological age, had simply responded by citing their common understanding of the term *media* rather than the specialized one required by their art teacher!

How, then, can we resolve this problem? One solution seems evident; we must teach students effective ways to learn and remember content area vocabulary words. The research of Shu, Anderson, and Zhang (1995) informs us that although incidental learning of word meanings occurs with narrative reading, this is not often the case with textbook reading. Furthermore, the plethora of research already cited in this book clearly supports Blachowicz and Fisher's (2002) third guideline: Effective teachers use instructional strategies that not only teach vocabulary effectively but model good word-learning behaviors. The strategies provided in this chapter offer some effective options for teachers to use.

Another problem teachers face when teaching content area vocabulary involves the question of exactly which words and how many words should one choose to teach. To help teachers decide which words to teach, Irvin, Buehl, and Radcliffe (2007) have outlined a plan of action for teaching content area vocabulary utilizing Allen's (1999) 10 decision-making questions, which are the following:

1. Which words are most important to understanding the text?

2. How much prior knowledge will students have about each word or related concept?

3. Is the word encountered frequently?

4. Does the word have multiple meanings?

5. Is the concept significant, and does it, therefore, require preteaching?

6. Which words can students figure out from context?

7. Can some words be grouped together to enhance the understanding of the concept?

8. What strategies can be used to help students integrate the word as well as related words into their lives?

9. How can students receive positive, productive repeated exposure to the word or concept?

10. How can students be encouraged to use the word or concept in meaningful ways and in multiple concepts?

Once the above questions have been answered, the teacher peruses the text the students will read to determine which words are essential for the students to learn and which are less essential. For example, in teaching the novel, *No Promises in the Wind,* by Irene Hunt, Roberta determined that it was essential for students to learn the word *sojourn,* since the trip the main characters take across the United States during the Great Depression was not simply a trip; it was a sojourn. And the word *dilapidated* needed to be taught as well, since the novel spoke of ramshackle houses, but it was also implied that the homeless of the Great Depression possessed dilapidated souls. The less-essential list would include those words that students might have some cursory knowledge of or that might occur on a list they would generate themselves. These words could be taught immediately after the selection was read or while it was being discussed. For those words that are deemed essential for students to know, the teacher can utilize any of the strategies presented in the following pages of this chapter.

Scaffolding Vocabulary Development

As discussed in Chapter 1 of this book, instructional scaffolding is a method by which teachers can support students' efforts to read and understand their texts by supplying them with specific and effective strategies for completing these tasks. Teachers can use the following strategies to scaffold their students' vocabulary development.

WORD CATEGORIZATION ACTIVITIES

Categorization is a method by which words are assigned to some category. In vocabulary categorization activities, students assign the concept words they are learning to appropriate categories and then justify and explain their decisions. According to Richardson and Morgan (2003), the explanation and discussion that takes place is a powerful way for students to learn and remember concept vocabulary words. Three prominent word categorization activities, the Word Association strategy and Open and Closed Word Sorts, are presented below.

Making Word Associations

This word categorization strategy focuses on helping students learn the concept word through the identification of synonyms and antonyms.

Steps for Making Word Associations

1. Use six to ten words from a unit.

2. Ask students to find three synonyms for each of the core words.

3. Ask students to find one antonym or nondefinition for each core word.

4. List the words in a sequence. Ask students to circle the word that does not belong and provide a reason for their choice.

5. As a follow-up activity, have students write a sentence using one or more of the words in bold text.

See Figure 2.1 for an example of the Word Association strategy for consumer science and Figure 2.2 for an example for social studies.

Directions: In each row, circle the term that does **not** define the word that is highlighted.

expansion	broadening	**diversification**	specialization	variation
contraction	deal	operation	**transaction**	contract
brochure	**prospectus**	leaflet	catalog	commercial
stockbroker	dealer	agent	negotiator	navigator
losses	principal	**capital**	assets	finances

Sentence: The **transaction** came as a result of the company's **diversification** process.

Figure 2.1   Example Word Association for Business or Consumer Science Unit: Investing

---

Directions: In each row, circle the term that does **not** define the word that is highlighted.

secular	worldly	material	lay	spiritual
viewpoint	perception	**perspective**	outlook	position
dialect	**vernacular**	stilted	idiom	lingo
ideal	idyllic	**utopian**	ultimate	dystopian
indulgence	luxury	excess	treat	necessity
rift	union	rupture	split	**schism**

Sentence: The **perspective** of Renaissance society was **secular** rather than religious.

Figure 2.2   Example Word Association for Social Studies Unit: Italy—Birthplace of the Renaissance

Word Sorts

The strategy of Word Sorts, developed by Gillet and Kita (1979), asks students to classify words into categories based on what they already know or have experienced about the words (prior knowledge). In the Word Sorts strategy, students use a list of key words identified by the teacher from the unit to be studied, examine the meanings of words, and then categorize the words according to features or similarities the words share. Again, as in the Word Association strategy discussed above, the power and effectiveness of the strategy lies in the discussion students have with one another as they examine the words (Gillet & Kita, 1979).

Content area teachers can use word sorts as a prereading or a postreading strategy. When it is used as a prereading strategy, students can use their prior knowledge to sort words and set a purpose for reading. When it is used as an after-reading strategy, students can reflect on what they learned and process their understandings on the text and concepts (Johns & Berglund, 2002). Either way, Word Sorts provide students a means to become more aware of the words used in the text.

There are two types of Word Sorts, the Closed Sort and the Open Sort, and both can be effectively used in any content area. In a Closed Sort, students are given the main categories into which they must sort the list of words; thus, this strategy is often considered easier, because students do not need to create their own categories. In an Open Sort, no categories are provided, and students must utilize critical, divergent, and inductive thinking to examine the meanings and relationships among the words and then create appropriate categories in which to place the listed words.

Steps for a Closed Word Sort

1. From a reading selection, select 15 to 20 key vocabulary words that can be sorted in three or four categories.

2. Next, select a name for each category, and list each category on the chalkboard, a transparency, or a sheet of paper in grid fashion with the categories listed in the top row of the grid.

3. Distribute the list of words to the students, and ask them to place the words in the appropriate categories on the grid. Remind students that they must justify the reasons for their choices.

See Figure 2.3 for an example of a Closed Word Sort for American literature and Figure 2.4 for an example of a Closed Word Sort for biology.

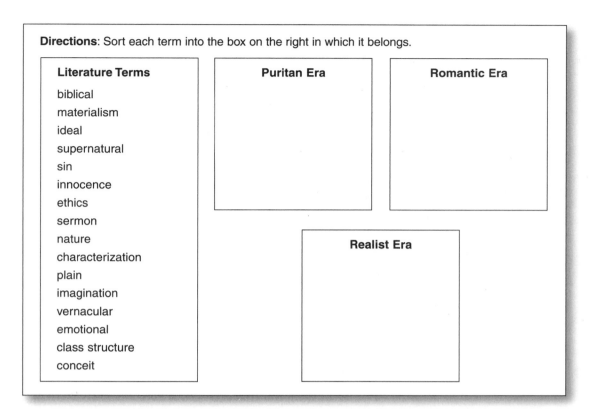

Figure 2.3   Example of Closed Word Sort for American Literature

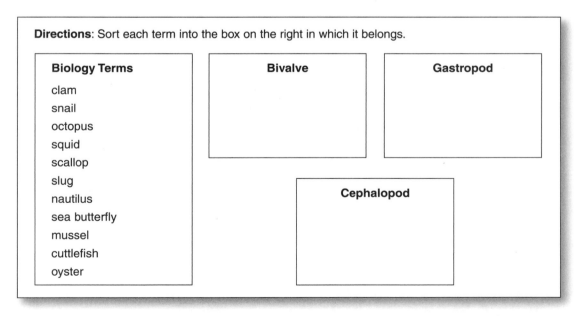

Figure 2.4   Example of Closed Word Sort for Biology

Steps for an Open Word Sort

1. From a reading selection, select 15 to 20 key vocabulary words that can be sorted into three or four categories.

2. Distribute the list to the students to study, and ask them to determine the word meanings and identify any relationships they see among the words in order to determine a set of three or four categories into which the words might fit.

3. Have students create a grid and write the categories they have chosen in the first row of the grid.

4. Finally, have the students complete the grid by placing each word in the appropriate category.

See Figure 2.5 for an example of an Open Word Sort for mathematics and Figure 2.6 for an example for music.

Directions: Survey the words, identify categories, and sort the list of words into the appropriate categories.

obtuse	trapezoid	parallelogram	quadrilateral	pentagon
rhombus	isosceles	decagon	rectangle	triangle
acute	polygon	hexagon	scalene	
octagon	equilateral	right	square	

Figure 2.5   Example of Open Word Sort for Mathematics

Directions: Survey the words, identify categories, and sort the list of words into the appropriate categories.

Armstrong	syncopation	written	rural	blues
piano	improvisation	ensemble	folk song	jazz
Joplin	spiritual	distorted	reprised strain	Harlem
prominent meter	ragtime	three phrases	sixteen measures	Waters

Figure 2.6   Example of Open Word Sort for Music

GRAPHIC REPRESENTATIONS

Graphic organizers help students associate an unfamiliar word with familiar related words by noting their spatial relationships. According to Ausubel (1978), if the elements of a concept are organized in an orderly fashion, students will learn them more easily, because they will see how the elements are related to one another. In addition, using a graphic organizer enables students to visualize and understand the meaning of terms, develops higher-level thinking skills, and creates meaning for the learner.

Concept of Definition

As discussed earlier in this chapter, learning content area vocabulary words is often difficult for students, since these words are usually very specialized in their meanings and reflect the concepts of the discipline itself. As a result, students need to learn more than just a brief phrase as the definition of a concept word. Instead, to gain a deep understanding of the meaning of a concept word, students need to identify the characteristics that illustrate the concept word as well as locate examples of it. A vocabulary strategy that fosters this kind of deep understanding of concept words and utilizes a graphic organizer to help students see the relationships of the various elements in the concept word is the Concept of Definition (Schwartz & Raphael, 1985). This strategy uses a graphic organizer to encourage students to delve into a concept word and become aware of the types of information that contribute to the meaning of a word. Students can then integrate this information into their own prior knowledge by generating a description and examples of the concept word.

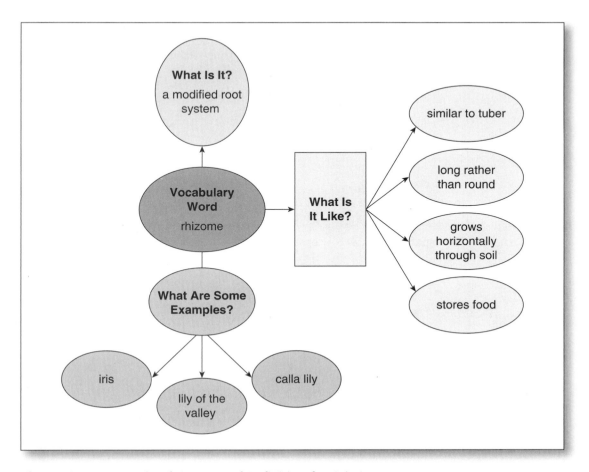

Figure 2.7   Example of Concept of Definition for Science

Steps for Concept of Definition

1. Present a new term or concept that students are to learn.

2. Place the word in the center of the Concept of Definition map.

3. Next, instruct students to consult their texts, a glossary, or a dictionary (individually or in small groups) to complete the remaining parts of the concept map, using the following guidelines:

   a. State the definition of the word in the section of the concept map labeled "What Is It?"

   b. Identify the word's characteristics or properties, and place these in the sections of the concept map labeled "What Is It Like?"

4. Have students brainstorm examples of the word from their own background knowledge. Tell them to place this information in the section of the concept map labeled "What Are Some Examples?"

Figure 2.7 shows how this strategy can be used in a science classroom, and Figure 2.8 shows an example for mathematics. Figure 2.16 on page 38 provides a reproducible master for the strategy.

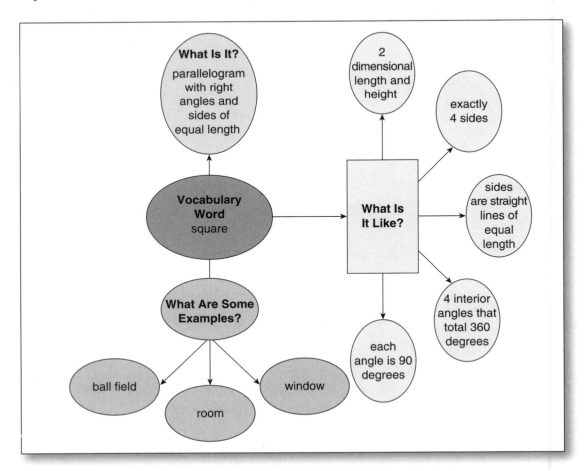

Figure 2.8   Example of Concept of Definition for Mathematics

A Variation of the Concept of Definition

The Concept of Definition Map variation (Tama & McClain, 2001) graphic organizer is a simplified variation of Schwartz and Raphael's Concept of Definition. This strategy asks students to define the term; use it in a sentence that provides a context clue, a synonym, an antonym, or a definition; and provide an illustration of the selected term. The use of a picture helps students visualize the meaning of the term. This strategy is especially effective in meeting the needs of visual or tactile learners. See Figure 2.9 for an example of how an adapted version of Tama and McClain's strategy can be utilized in a technology or music classroom. Figure 2.17 on page 39 provides a reproducible master for the Concept of Definition Map variation.

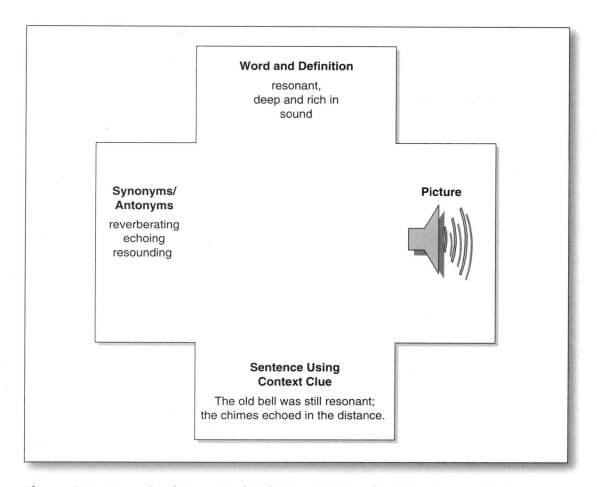

Figure 2.9   Example of Concept of Definition Variation for Technology or Music

THE WRITING CONNECTION

Reading comprehension and long-term recall of subject matter and vocabulary can be taught and improved through writing. In fact, students are more likely to remember words if they incorporate them into their writing. Teachers can use a variety of writing activities to introduce or reinforce vocabulary words. Some examples are as follows:

1. Write a story, song, or editorial using 15 of the vocabulary words.
2. Write a poem that defines the term by using synonyms.
3. Write a recipe that defines a term.
4. Write a story problem to find the definition to a term.
5. Use four or five vocabulary terms to create a business card (see Figure 2.10).

Word list: assets, consultation, commission, defraud, forestall, incur, liability, subsidiary

> Personal Injury and Medical Malpractice
>
> When you **incur** serious financial **liabilities** due to injuries, **forestall** future problems by contacting
>
> Robert Black and Associates
> **773-555-0146**
> **221 RIVER ROAD**
> **CHICAGO, IL**
> http://www.example.com
>
> Free Initial **Consultation**   We Guarantee Results

Figure 2.10   Example of a Business Card Utilizing the Writing Connection

In addition, Word Mysteries, Possible Sentences, and Story Impressions are strategies that require students to use the new vocabulary terms to write paragraphs and sentences.

Word Mysteries

The Word Mystery is an interactive form of a detective story. Each case will entertain the students and promote such higher-level thinking skills as inference, deductive reasoning, and drawing conclusions. In order to solve a mystery, students need to be able to make connections among clues that you provide and with which they may or may not have previously been familiar.

Steps for Word Mysteries

1. Determine the word or concept you want students to come to understand as they solve the mystery. Use the concepts of *who, what, why,* and *where* as a basis for the question you want to ask about the word or concept.

2. Create a case based on the meanings and functions of the word.

3. Write the question and provide three to four clues on one side of a sheet of paper.

4. Write the answer on the other side of the paper.

See Figure 2.11 for an example of a Word Mystery for biology and Figure 2.12 for an example for social studies.

The Case:

This animal lives in fresh and salt water, in damp soil and among vegetation. It may seem complex; however, it is one of the simplest forms of animal life.

The Question:

What is the name of the animal and how is it unique?

The Clues:

1. It is distinguished by the absence of a nonliving membrane or cell wall.

2. Its external layer is an integral part of its existence.

3. It reproduces asexually by division, sometimes called binary fusion.

The Answer: the amoeba; some are parasites of animals, including man

---

Figure 2.11   Example of Word Mystery for Biology

The Case:

He is a military leader who gave hope to thousands during the Depression by working tirelessly to create reforms in labor laws and housing. Although he did not fight in World War II, he delegated power to others to fight.

The Question:

Who is the man and what did he do?

The Clues:

1. The man governed New York.

2. He was an expert in creating political policies.

3. He worked with Winston Churchill.

4. He worked to launch the United Nations.

The Answer: Franklin Delano Roosevelt, President of the United States

---

Figure 2.12   Example of Word Mystery for Social Studies

Possible Sentences

Possible Sentences, created by Moore and Moore (1986) was designed as a vehicle to help students decipher unfamiliar vocabulary words they might discover in their content area reading assignments. Utilized before the students begin reading, the strategy asks students to survey a list of words and then to make predictions about the meaning of the selection they will read based upon what they already know or can assume about the relationships among the words. They then combine the words to create a series of "possible sentences" about the selection to be read.

Steps for Possible Sentences

1. List 10 to 15 concept words that are essential to the understanding of the selection to be read. It is important to include a few words that are familiar to students as well as those that students do not know.

2. Next ask students to choose two words from the list and write a sentence that they think might appear in the selection they will read.

3. Record the sentence, underlining the key words used, exactly as the students dictate it, even though it might not reflect an exact representation of the word's meaning or the text's content.

4. Continue this process until all the concept words have been used in sentences. If some words are completely unfamiliar to students, encourage them to guess at a meaning, reminding them that these are "possible sentences." (Note: Words may be utilized in more than one sentence as long as the new sentence presents a new concept.)

5. When all the sentences have been completed, instruct students to verify the authenticity of their sentences by reading the assigned selection. Buehl (2001) suggests that students evaluate each sentence by determining whether

   a. the sentence is true, because the text supports the prediction made in the sentence.

   b. the sentence is false, because the text provides a different use of the terms.

   c. no decision can be made, because the text does not clearly deal with the prediction made.

Figure 2.13 provides an example of Possible Sentences for health.

Terms:

protein   vegetarian   cholesterol   nutrients   mineral   fortified

Possible Sentences:

1. Lowering *cholesterol* is now possible by taking nutritional supplements that have *nutrients.*
2. All their natural *mineral* make-up is *preservative* free.
3. *Vegetarians* can now opt for low *carbohydrates* and still be healthy.
4. Consumers are demanding healthier beverages that are *fortified* with *proteins.*

Figure 2.13   Example of Possible Sentences for Health

Story Impressions

The Story Impression strategy (McGinley & Denner, 1987) asks students to use clue words associated with important ideas and events in the content area to write their own version of the material prior to reading. Story Impressions help readers understand and make predictions about the terms and information before they read, help them make possible connections to the material, and help improve comprehension skills by providing them with fragments of the actual content. After reading a set of clues, students are asked to make sense of them and use them to compose a paragraph of their own in advance of reading the content.

Steps for Story Impressions

Before Teaching

1. Preview a beginning or essential portion section of the text.
2. Identify a series of terms or two- to three-word phrases that are related to significant concepts.
3. List the words or phrases in the order that students will find them in the text.
4. Create a work sheet with the terms arranged in a vertical column connected by arrows to indicate the order.

To Teach

1. Students can work with a partner or in small groups to brainstorm possible connections among the terms and to make predictions about the content and the meaning of unfamiliar words.
2. Continuing in their pairs or small groups, students work together to write a paragraph that represents their interpretations of the words.
   a. Students must use all of the words in these paragraphs.

   b. Students must integrate the terms into the paragraph in the order in which they appear in the list.

3. After writing their paragraphs, students read the text.

4. After reading the text, students read their paragraphs and mark the terms they used accurately.

5. If needed, students can write a second paragraph to compare and contrast the examples.

See Figure 2.14 for an example of a Story Impression for biology and Figure 2.15 for an example for literature. Figure 2.18 on page 40 provides a reproducible master for this strategy.

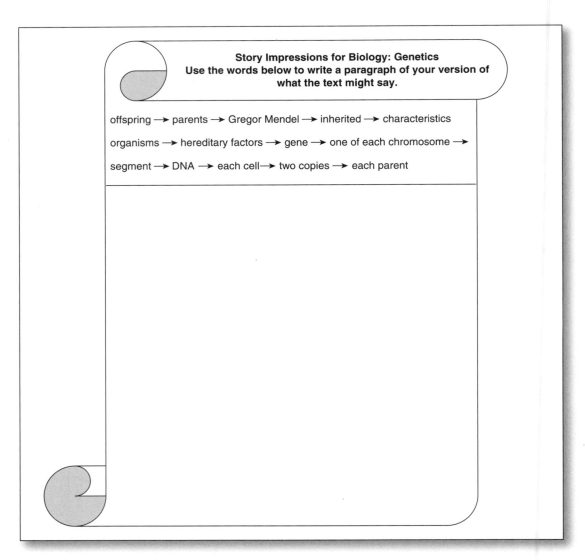

Story Impressions for Biology: Genetics
Use the words below to write a paragraph of your version of what the text might say.

offspring → parents → Gregor Mendel → inherited → characteristics

organisms → hereditary factors → gene → one of each chromosome →

segment → DNA → each cell → two copies → each parent

Figure 2.14   Example of a Story Impression for Biology

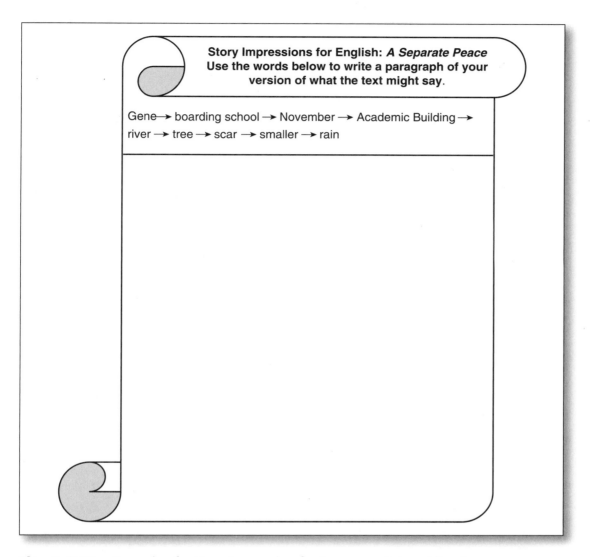

Figure 2.15   Example of a Story Impression for Language Arts or Literature

CHAPTER SUMMARY

As noted at the beginning of this chapter, the end product of both recreational and informational reading is comprehension. Furthermore, since vocabulary knowledge makes up much as 70% to 80% of comprehension, one cannot deny the critical importance of helping students acquire, learn, and retain that vocabulary. To that end, Chapter 2 provides a myriad of strategies to foster vocabulary acquisition and knowledge in all content areas.

CONCEPT OF DEFINITION

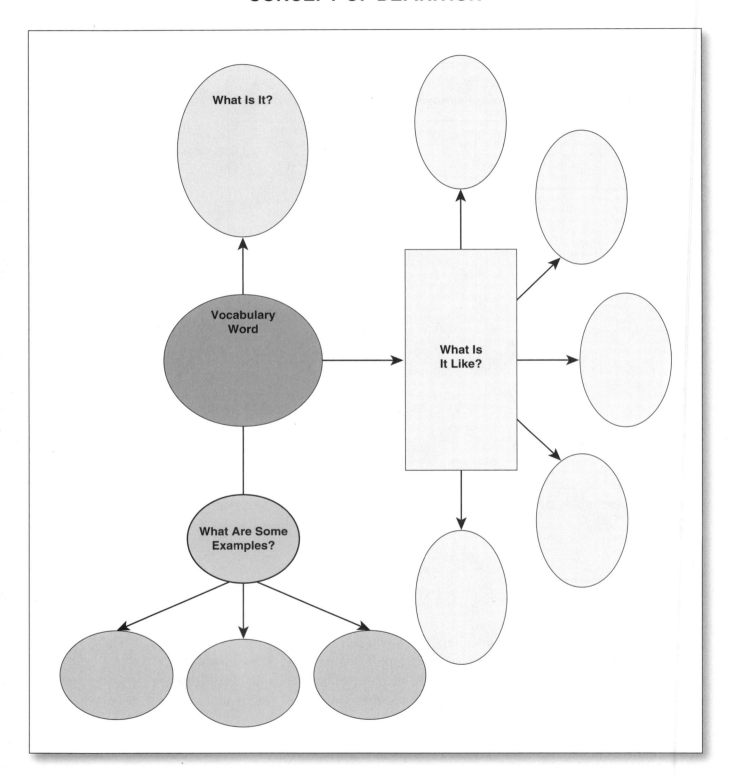

Figure 2.16   Reproducible Master for Concept of Definition

CONCEPT OF DEFINITION MAP VARIATION

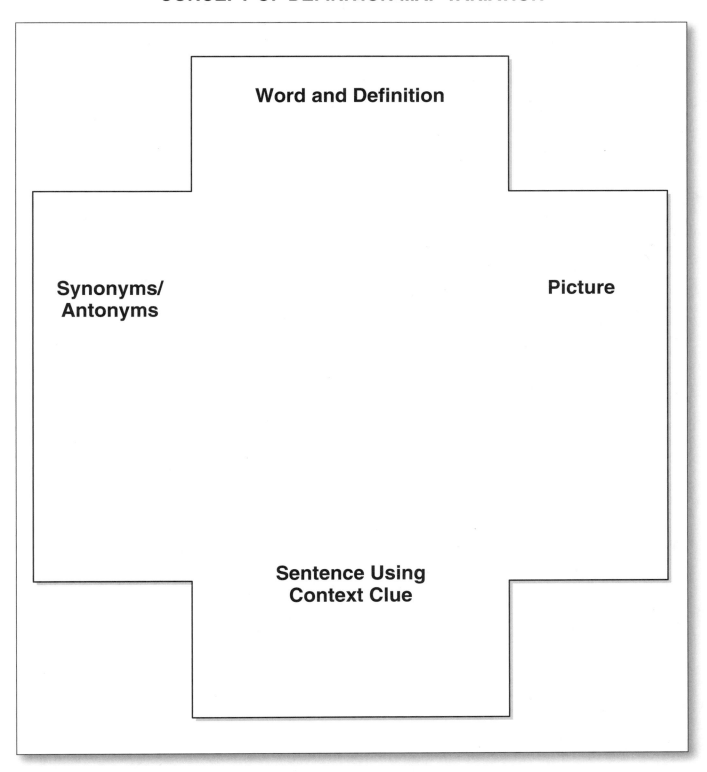

Figure 2.17   Reproducible Master for Concept of Definition Map Variation

STORY IMPRESSION

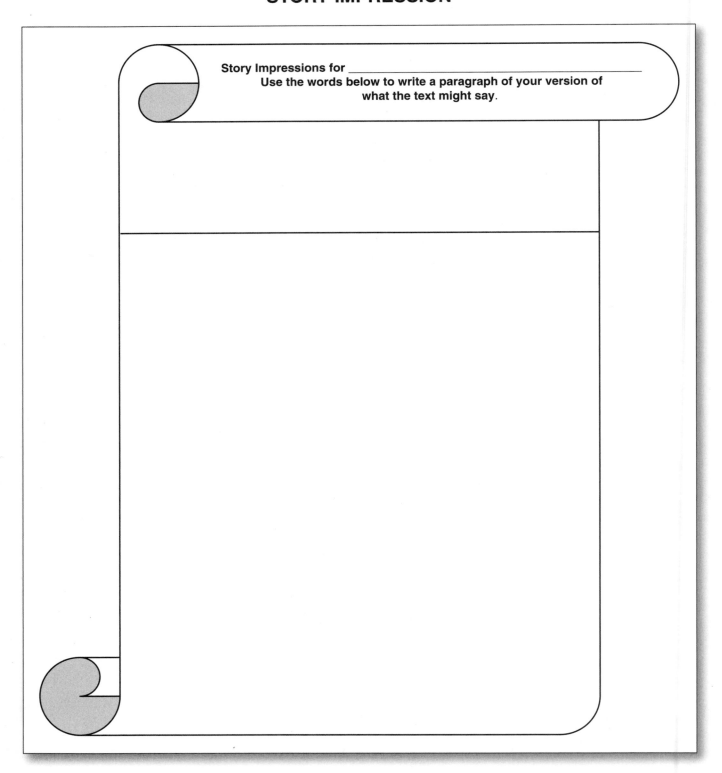

Story Impressions for _____
Use the words below to write a paragraph of your version of
what the text might say.

Figure 2.18 Reproducible Master for Story Impression

CHAPTER 3

Reading to Learn in Content Area Disciplines

Learning is not attained by chance; it must be sought
for with ardor and attended to with diligence.

Abigail Adams

READING IN SPECIFIC CONTENT AREA DISCIPLINES

As discussed in Chapter 1, the reading processes and skills required of students differ from content area discipline to content area discipline. When reading for English or language arts classes, students are required to read both narrative and expository texts. These texts cover a variety of subjects, such as grammar and composition, and include novels, short stories, poetry, biographies, and autobiographies. Words in these texts may have denotative and connotative meanings, they may be specialized vocabulary words like oxymorons and acronyms, and some terms may reflect word meanings that change.

Furthermore, in order for students to effectively respond to their English or language arts texts, they must be able carry out a variety of tasks. Roe, Stoodt-Hill, and Burns (2007) tell us that for narrative texts, students need to be able to

1. interpret what has been read.

2. describe what has been read.

3. discriminate among texts based on type, author, theme, etc.

4. understand and interpret the writing's mood, tone, and voice.

5. relate the information from one reading to understand another.

6. make personal connections to the reading.

7. respond to the reading creatively.

In order to effectively understand expository texts in English and language arts, Roe et al. (2007) state that students must be able to identify the

1. author's purpose.

2. author's argument or thesis or bias toward the topic and the reader.

3. details used to support the argument.

4. organizational pattern used by the author to present the material.

5. specialized vocabulary utilized.

Reading mathematics texts requires skills that differ in some respects from those needed to read English or language arts texts. As discussed in Chapter 1, mathematics texts introduce a concept, explain it, provide an example, and, finally, pose a problem to solve that illustrates the concept. According to Roe et al. (2007), mathematics texts contain highly compressed language of a mix of words and symbols, where symbols commonly represent words. Furthermore, common words often assume a specialized meaning. Think, for example, of the word *power* as it pertains to mathematics as opposed to how it pertains to physical education or social studies. In addition, the prose in math is dense and contains more ideas per line and page than prose in other content areas. Furthermore, the text is most often written in a sequential or demonstration pattern, and main ideas usually appear in the chapter title or subheadings.

If students are to successfully read and comprehend their mathematics textbooks, they must be able clarify, paraphrase, and elaborate on what the text says. In effect, that requires students to comprehend and remember technical, specialized vocabulary as well as identify and make sense of the symbols, signs, abbreviations, formulas, figures, and graphs they encounter as they read. Therefore, they must be taught several of the vocabulary strategies discussed in Chapter 2, especially Concept of Definition and its variation as well as Word Mysteries. Finally, students must be cautioned to read slowly, so they can comprehend both the linguistic and schematic concepts presented.

Science texts also require specialized reading skills. According to Roe et al. (2007), science texts are often written in a terse, dense style similar to other scientific writing, and the text patterns are usually cause-effect, definition-example, comparison-contrast, or problem-solution. (See Figure 1.2 for a review of these text structures.) Furthermore, the text will usually introduce important information with a thesis paragraph and then provide detailed support in following paragraphs. In addition, students' visual literacy is in demand, since science texts often have a multitude of pictures, charts, and tables, which provide additional details about the topic. Unfortunately, however, while vocabulary is crucial to text understanding, explicit definitions of all terms used are not always provided in the text.

Thus, in order for students to effectively maneuver through their science reading, it is important for them to understand how text structures will facilitate their comprehension, a technique that is easily taught utilizing the Text Structure strategy discussed in Chapter 1. In addition, since science texts contain technical, specialized vocabulary terms that may not be defined in student friendly terms, students need to be taught a variety of the vocabulary strategies presented in Chapter 2. Also, Roe et al. (2007) suggest that students read the text slowly in order to process the dense concepts as well the diagrams, graphs, tables, charts, symbols, and formulas presented. Finally, students should be encouraged to reread the text more than once so they can take careful notes and process the dense concepts presented.

Social studies texts are written in a journalistic, factual, precise style where main ideas are presented and then embellished upon in later paragraphs. In addition, maps, tables, and photographs, which require students to use their visual literacy skills, are provided to further support the concepts presented. Furthermore, as with science reading, an understanding of text structure patterns such as cause-effect, definition-example, comparison-contrast, and problem-solution, as well as the idea of presenting concepts in chronological or time order, facilitates student understanding. Finally, chapters and subheadings are usually organized around concepts such as "exploration" or "culture" or "inventions" and, as a result, require that students make use of their prior knowledge about such topics.

For success in reading social studies texts, Roe et al. (2007) remind us that students must comprehend 75% of the ideas and 90% of the concept vocabulary included in each reading selection. Therefore, according to Roe et al. (2007) and Hickey (1990) they must be able to do the following:

1. Acquire and retain relevant concepts and information

2. Understand cause and effect relationships

3. Distinguish between fact and opinion

4. Separate relevant from irrelevant information, evaluating ideas for authenticity

5. Evaluate propaganda

6. Understand ideas and viewpoints of others

7. Think critically and creatively to develop new attitudes, perspectives, and values and to make decisions

8. Read critically about events and why they happened

The areas of fine arts and vocational arts provide yet different reading challenges for students to meet. In these classes, in addition to reading regular textbooks, which, according to Roe et al. (2007), are written in a concise expository or narrative style and filled with dense concepts, students are often asked to read primary sources such as articles, pamphlets, memos, and reference and instruction manuals as well as to view films, CD-ROMs, and other electronic media, the understanding of which requires both visual literacy and critical thinking. Furthermore, texts in these content areas often contain specialized, technical words and expressions such as *obbligato* and *aria* in music, *chiaroscuro* in art, *accounts receivable* in business, *miter* in woodworking, or *pressure foot* in fashion and design. However, in most instances, neither effective context clues nor clear definitions are provided.

For successful comprehension of textbooks in fine arts and vocational arts, students must have a variety of skills, many of them relating to the ability to solve problems. In effect, Roe et al. (2007) tell us, students must utilize a flexible reading rate that incorporates both skimming and scanning and reading critically to locate information; interpreting charts, diagrams, scales, legends, illustrations, graphics, scripts, and scores; and following directions to visualize and implement the information in performances or projects. In effect, students in these content areas need to be able to apply the ideas they read about to actual real life situations.

As discussed above, various processes and skills are required for successful comprehension of the narration and exposition found in the various content area disciplines. In addition, each of those content disciplines presents certain comprehension challenges as well. While the following sections will provide a series of strategies that will equip students to become strategic learners, we first need to understand how to best help students effectively learn these strategies. Peterson, Caverly, Nicholson, O'Neal, and Cusenbary (2000) note that for students to effectively learn a new strategy, they must be taught how, why, and when to use it.

Winograd and Hare (1988) have set forth a series of five critical elements that should guide the direct explanation of any new strategy. First, each step of the new strategy must be carefully explained so it makes meaningful sense. Next, its benefits must be clarified, so the students understand why they need to learn the new strategy. Then, the strategy must be modeled in a step-by-step fashion so students know how it works. Once the strategy has been modeled, the students must understand the circumstances under which the strategies they are learning are most effective. Finally, they must take time to reflect on how well the strategies work for them.

Once students have been introduced to the new strategy, teachers should utilize the Gradual Release of Responsibility Model developed by Pearson and Gallagher (1983) as a way of helping students acquire the strategy. This process begins with the teacher demonstrating and modeling the steps of a strategy using an actual piece of text to illustrate each step. Next, in pairs or small groups and with teacher support, students practice the strategy. Finally, when students become proficient in the use of the strategy with teacher and/or peer support, they are ready to use the strategy independently. To effectively teach new strategies, Roe et al. (2007) have developed a plan of action, which is outlined below.

1. First, engage students by motivating them, activating their interest, and fostering their prior knowledge. At this point, introduce the strategy, giving it a name and explaining how and why students will find it is valuable for learning.

2. Second, model the strategy for students using text the students will use in class.

3. Next, students practice using the strategy themselves until they can comfortably apply it independently.

4. Finally, once students can independently utilize the strategy correctly, they should be encouraged to use it whenever it is merited.

SCAFFOLDING READING IN SPECIFIC CONTENT AREAS

The following section of this text is devoted to a discussion of strategies that can be used in all content area disciplines. These sections are divided into four sections: (1) questioning strategies, (2) note-taking and summary strategies, (3) study guide strategies, and (4) critical response strategies.

Questioning Strategies

Delores Durkin (1979) noted that, as teachers, we use questioning more than any other strategy to determine whether or not our students are learning. As a result, we often dominate the questioning process by generating all the questions and requiring our students to generate only a few (Armbruster et al., 1991; Busching & Slesinger, 1995). Furthermore, studies by Cazden (1986, 1988), Dillon (1988), and Mehan (1979) tell us that the majority of the questioning that occurs in classrooms follows the IRE cycle: **I**nitiate, **R**espond, **E**valuate, wherein the teacher initiates the question, and when the students respond to the question, the teacher decides whether the answer is right or wrong. However, according to Mehan, this format of inquiry leads to a passive learning environment when, in fact, our classrooms should be active places where students are engaged in their learning. To assure an active learning environment, Crapse (1995) suggests that we encourage students to generate their own questions. The following strategies provide some ways we can foster the question-generating abilities of our students.

Question-Answer Relationship Strategy (QARS)

As teachers, Sharon and I have long suspected that students have difficulty answering the questions they encounter at the end of text chapters, in class discussions, and on examinations, because they lack a process to follow for determining how to answer such questions. Raphael, Au, and Highfield (2006) posit that students need to understand that, basically, questions can be found in two places: "in the book" and "in my head." The "in the book" category contains two types of questions: (1) the "right there," or textually explicit question that is found easily in one place in the text, and (2) the "think and search," or the textually implicit question, which students must think about and peruse several sections of the text to answer. And, the "in my head" category also contains two types: (1) "author and you" and (2) "on your own" questions, which students must answer by processing and applying what they know and have learned and then transferring their knowledge to real life applications. See Figure 3.1 for an example of QAR for science.

Right There Questions

1. Chloroplasts contain a green material called what?
2. Through what part of the plant does water enter?

Think and Search Questions

1. What elements do plants require in order to successfully complete the process of photosynthesis?
2. Can photosynthesis occur in all layers of a plant leaf? Why?

Author and You Questions

1. Why do you think there are spaces between the lower leaf cells?
2. Why do you think the leaves change color in the fall?

On Your Own Questions

1. Write an equation that shows the process of photosynthesis.
2. Circle the side of the equation that shows the waste products.

Figure 3.1   Example of QAR for Science: Photosynthesis

Steps for QARS

1. Introduce the QAR strategy by defining and explaining the question types and providing an example of each. It is especially beneficial during this step to utilize examples from the texts students will be studying.

2. Once students clearly understand and can easily differentiate among the types of questions, assign them a short piece of text to read.

3. Using the text read, develop a set of QAR questions, and guide students through the process of answering each type of QAR question. At the end of this step, students should be able to clearly identify each of the four QAR question types.

4. Continue practice of the QAR strategy, increasing the number of questions for each type until students can clearly differentiate among the types and can identify them with ease.

5. Finally, when students can carry out the QAR strategy independently, they should be encouraged to use it when reading all assignments.

Questioning the Author

Questioning the Author (Beck, McKeown, Hamilton, & Kucan, 1997) is an effective strategy for helping students focus on their content area reading assignment, because it encourages them to interact with their reading and create meaning from it by taking time to analyze the author's purpose rather than merely reading what the text says. This strategy addresses a problem students often encounter when they discover that a text is not user friendly for them, either because they lack the appropriate level of prior knowledge they need to understand the concepts presented, or because the information in the text may not be explained as fully as students need. As a result, the text may be confusing if not incomprehensible to the student.

In order to combat this problem, Beck et al. (1997) have developed a strategy wherein teachers develop a series of questions or queries to serve as discussion prompts to guide students along the path to becoming responsible for their thinking and thus able to construct meaning for themselves. As teachers utilize the Question the Author strategy, they not only act as facilitators and guides but also initiate questions and sometimes even respond to them, all the while making certain that they are upholding the goals of the strategy, which are to help students (1) construct meaning from the text's content, (2) transcend the words on the page, and (3) make connections to real life experiences.

Steps for Questioning the Author

1. First, read the assigned text to determine the major concepts students should learn as well as any problems that might hinder their understanding of these concepts, such as text complexity or difficulty.

2. Next, divide the text into segments for student reading, determining at what points in the text the students will stop reading and begin discussing the question posed to the author. A way to effectively segment text is to pay attention to where major concepts occur or where difficult or confusing text emerges and segment the text at those points.

3. Once the text is segmented, the questions to be asked of the author are developed. These queries are designed to be used while students are reading and should help them focus on the quality and depth of their understanding of the text as well as facilitate discussion and interaction between students. Beck et al. (1997) describe three levels of queries: (1) initiating queries, (2) follow-up queries, which are designed to be used with expository text, and (3) narrative queries, which are designed to be used with narrative text. Examples and a fuller explanation of these queries are found in Figure 3.2.

4. In order to prepare students to question the author effectively, help students discover as well as understand who the author of the text is. This is best accomplished by asking students to think of the author as a participant in their discussion by posing questions such as, "Who is talking to you in this book?" "What expertise does he/she have?" "Why do you think the author wanted to write this text?"

5. As soon as students can identify who the author is, they are ready to begin to effectively question that author by utilizing the self-questioning process. You must first model this process by choosing a passage from the text and

proceeding to think through the reading aloud, noting what made the reading easy, difficult, or confusing, and identifying what concepts the author expects the reader to know and understand.

6. As the strategy progresses, maintain an active role by asking open-ended questions, affirming key points, paraphrasing or summarizing student commentaries, and even presenting supplementary information to clarify any material that may be unclear.

7. As students become comfortable in using this strategy, they can segment their text and begin to generate appropriate queries.

See Figure 3.2 for a list of queries to use in Questioning the Author.

Expository Queries

Goal of Query	Possible Queries
Initiate a discussion	1. What do you think the author is trying to say in this reading?
	2. What do you think is the message the author is giving you?
	3. What do you think the author is really talking about?

Follow up to focus on
  1. what the author meant.
  2. making connections.
  3. why the author presents certain information and ideas.
	1. What do you think the author means in his text?
	2. Do you think the author explains her ideas clearly in her writing?
	3. Does what the author says in this passage make sense with what he has said before?
	4. How does what the author says here help you connect to what you have learned before?
	5. Why do you think the author includes the information she does?

Narrative Queries

Goal of Query	Possible Queries
Examine characters and their motivations	1. Based on what you have read, what is the author telling you about the character and her situation? 2. What hints can you get from what the author has told you to help you predict what the character will do next?
Examine how the plot is crafted	1. What information does the author present that helps you figure out that things have changed for the character? 2. How does the author bring the events in the plot to a close?

Figure 3.2 Question the Author Queries

SOURCE: Based on suggestions for questions provided by Beck, McKeown, Hamilton, & Kucan (1997, pp. 37–42).

Bloom's Taxonomy and the Discussion Cube

Bloom's Taxonomy (Bloom, 1984) is an effective strategy that gives teachers a precise language for communicating the outcomes of their learning instruction, helps students identify different levels of thinking and questioning, and is a valuable tool for building students' critical and creative thinking skills. In the taxonomy, the acts of recalling and reporting knowledge are seen as less sophisticated than the alternatives of translating information into new forms; however, students just embarking in a new discipline ought to be encouraged to practice the full array of higher-order thinking skills. Once they have those skills, they have the ability to apply and transfer their knowledge in different contexts.

Teachers can use Bloom's Taxonomy for a variety purposes, including class discussions, test questions, activities, assignments, groups, and as a means of teaching students how to identify and write different kinds of questions. Based on the taxonomy, Figure 3.3 illustrates diverse levels of questions that could be used to study the work of the artist Pablo Picasso. In addition, teachers can create menus like the one in Figure 3.4 to provide a range of different activities or assignments based on the taxonomy.

Pablo Picasso

Level	Trigger Words	Question Starters
KNOWLEDGE Recalling appropriate, previously learned information	list, identify, name, tell, recall, recount, who, when, where	Can you name the city where Picasso developed his talent? What was his famous mural called?
COMPREHENSION Understanding the meaning of informational materials	summarize, estimate, discuss, describe, explain, distinguish	How would you explain the Cubist technique? How would you describe the way he portrayed ballerinas?
APPLICATION Applying previously learned knowledge to new and unfamiliar situations	demonstrate, illustrate, examine, show, classify, relate	How would you illustrate the proportions of one of his sculptures? How would you demonstrate the technique of Cubism?
ANALYSIS Examining and trying to understand the organizational structure of information	compare, infer, consider, investigate, examine	How did Cubism differ from Synthetic Cubism? Why were his paintings controversial?
SYNTHESIS Applying prior knowledge and skills to combine elements into a new pattern	modify, create, rearrange, design, plan, compose, formulate	How would you create a postcard that illustrates Cubism? How would you prepare a time line that illustrates his accomplishments?
EVALUATION Judging according to some set of criteria, without real right or wrong answers	decide, rank, judge, select, assess, convince, determine	Which of his Rose Period paintings was most influential? Which of his sculptures is best known?

Figure 3.3   Example of Bloom's Taxonomy Levels for Art Appreciation

Menu for Shakespeare's *Romeo and Juliet*

KNOWLEDGE	APPLICATION	SYNTHESIS	COMPREHENSION
Recall how the fight started in the first act of the play.	Write a bio-poem illustrating one of the character's traits.	Write a newspaper article describing a conflict in one or more scenes.	Write a journal entry retelling what happens when Romeo and Juliet meet.
ANALYSIS	**EVALUATION**	**EVALUATION**	**ANALYSIS**
Create a Venn diagram comparing two characters.	Write an editorial explaining who was responsible for their deaths.	Write a journal entry describing one of the character's flaws and explain how it affected him or her.	Write a plan so Romeo and Juliet can be together.
COMPREHENSION	**APPLICATION**	**SYNTHESIS**	**KNOWLEDGE**
Write a letter from a parent explaining why Romeo and Juliet should not marry.	Write two paragraphs explaining how one of Romeo's conflicts related to an issue in the play.	Create a maze to illustrate the time frame of the conflicts in the story.	List the members of both families.

Figure 3.4   Example of Bloom's Taxonomy Questions for English/Language Arts

Teachers can also use the cubing strategy (Cowan & Cowan, 1980) to create a discussion cube based on Bloom's Taxonomy by following these steps:

Steps to Create a Discussion Cube

1. Create a cube. (Use a small tissue box covered with paper, or see the reproducible master for a cube in Figure 3.20 on page 70.)

2. On the sides, print the following terms, one on each side:
   a. Describe
   b. Compare/contrast
   c. Associate
   d. Analyze
   e. Apply
   f. Argue for or against

3. Ask students to respond verbally or in written form to one or more sides of the cube based on their ability or their choice. This strategy is especially effective for differentiating the curriculum.

See Figure 3.5 for an example of cubing for the topic of manifest destiny.

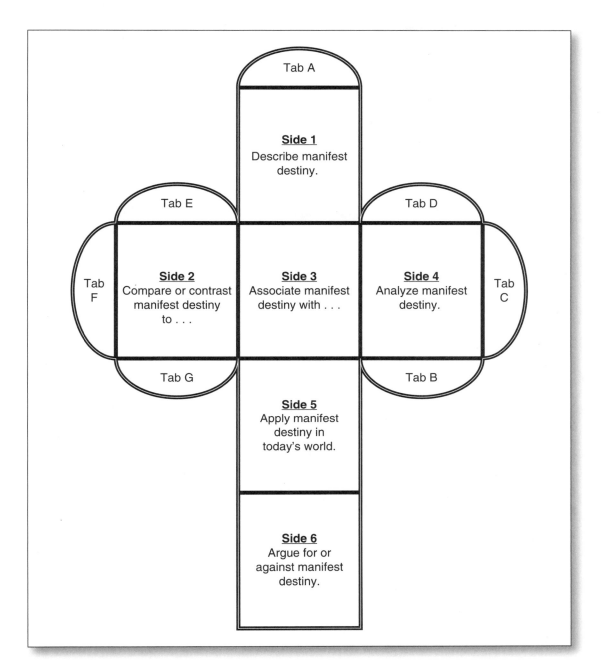

Figure 3.5 Example of Cubing for Concept of Manifest Destiny

SOURCE: Cube form adapted from R. G. Meyer and Southern Regional ETTC.

Note-Taking and Summarizing Strategies

Framed Outlines

As discussed above, sometimes the texts students are asked to read are not user friendly, because students lack the appropriate level of prior knowledge needed to understand the concepts presented, because the information in the texts is not explained as fully as students need, or because the readability of the text is above the reading level of the students, thus making the reading task complex and difficult. In addition, sometimes students simply have difficulty determining what is important in the texts they read or in the lectures they hear. Finally, this situation is often complicated by the fact that some students are novices when it comes to note taking. To help students who face this learning dilemma, Tama and McClain (2001) developed the Note Taking Framed Outlines strategy, which provides a structured framework of the critical ideas in a reading assignment or lecture with blanks where critical points exist, so that students can navigate through the reading or lecture and fill in the critical ideas as they read or hear them. Tama and McClain (2001) point out that using the Note Taking Framed Outlines strategy is an excellent way to introduce students to the note-taking process, since it helps them identify key ideas and supporting details.

Steps for Note Taking Framed Outlines

1. First choose a segment of text or a lecture, and prepare a framed outline that includes the major ideas and critical details that the student should remember.

2. Second, model the strategy, explaining the process carefully. Tama and McClain (2001) suggest that the modeling procedure be carried out during a lecture with the teacher stopping to fill in the blanks in the framed outline on a transparency, so the students can see how the strategy works.

3. Once students understand the process, they may complete assigned framed outlines independently.

See Figure 3.6 for an example of the use of this strategy in an art lesson.

Surrealism is a style of _____ that makes use of _____ _____ _____ visual that has been created from musings of the _____ _____. In surrealistic art, the artist does not attempt to make the artwork he or she produces _____ _____.

This art form, similar to art created in the _____ _____ _____ _____ movement, was founded by _____ in _____ and was most popular in _____, where it attracted members of the chaotic _____ _____. It was deeply influenced by the _____ _____ _____ _____ _____ _____. The artists who made up the Surrealist circle were the best-known Surrealist artist _____ _____ as well as lesser known artists such as _____ _____, _____ _____, _____ _____, _____ _____, and _____ _____.

Figure 3.6   Example of Note Taking Framed Outline for Art

Power Notes

Power Notes is an organizational tool that can help students differentiate between and then prioritize the main and supporting ideas in a text, can assist students in looking for relationships within the material, and can guide them in taking consistent notes from textbooks or classroom presentations (Buehl, 2001). Using this strategy, students think about the information in the text, determine what level it belongs to, and outline the information in hierarchal order. Main ideas or topics are assigned a Power 1 rating, and subtopics, examples, or attributes are assigned Power 2s, 3s, or 4s.

Steps in Power Notes

1. Begin instruction by providing the following basic outline model for students:

   Power 1. Main idea

   Power 2. Details or support of Power 1

   Power 3. Details or support of Power 2

2. Illustrate specific examples of Power Notes by choosing categories students recognize. Indicate how the powers relate to each other. The following example applies to car maintenance:

   Power 1. Maintaining a car

   Power 2. Tune-ups

   Power 3. Oil changes

   Power 3. Coolants

   Power 2. Maintenance checks

   Power 3. Tires

   Power 3. Brakes

3. Provide students with opportunities to practice using Power Notes to categorize information and explore relationships in a unit of study. To do this, you can write the terms on index cards and let students organize the cards to create an outline according to powers and relationships. For example, cards in a biology unit on health could include a Power 1 (nutrition), Power 2s (carbohydrates, fruits, vegetables, vitamins, and minerals), and Power 3s (bread, pasta, apples, beans, calcium, sodium, fat soluble, and water soluble).

You can also ask small groups of students to read one or more paragraphs of the text to create their own Power Notes, and then ask them to compare their notes with those of other groups. Power Notes can also be an effective means to help students organize and construct a well-written paragraph or essay or to prepare an answer for an essay test. Power Notes gives students a means to analyze their writing in terms of structure and development of ideas. See Figure 3.7 for an example of a power outline and a paragraph for social studies. Students could further elaborate each point in this figure by adding Power 3 and Power 4 details to flesh out their writing.

Question: How did President John Kennedy affect the civil rights movement?

Power 1. Endorsed the movement

Power 2. Met with civil rights leaders in SCLC and NAACP

Power 2. Violence increased need for backing movement

Power 2. Prepared a civil rights bill

President John Kennedy privately supported the civil rights movement. He met with leaders of the Southern Christian Leadership Conference and the National Association for the Advancement of Colored People to promote their efforts to ensure equal opportunities for all people. When violence broke out against the Freedom Riders in 1961 and against peaceful protesters in Birmingham, Alabama, in 1963, the president publicly backed the movement. Later that year, the president prepared a civil rights bill that offered protection for African Americans seeking rights to vote, eat out, and have equal education. President Kennedy's decisions reversed eight years of opposition to the civil rights movement.

Figure 3.7   Example of Power Notes for Social Studies

In effect, Power Notes offer an easy method for prioritizing information, understanding relationships, and clarifying information as well as help students process what they read in order to outline key points to study for an essay test or to write a paragraph or an essay.

Magnet Summary

Summaries, as we know, help students crystallize what they have read into its main points. In effect, they must read, comprehend, and then restate what has been said in a more concise way, using their own words. The greatest task students often face in writing summaries, however, is that they must be able to determine what ideas and details in the reading are important enough to be included. It requires them to categorize details, eliminate insignificant information, generalize information, and use clear, concise language to communicate the essence of what they have read. Needless to say, being able to decipher important information from a reading is the first step to good note taking. Thus teaching students to summarize materials they have read will better equip them to read and understand their content area reading. Vacca and Vacca (2008) provide a basic set of rules, adapted from the work of Kintsch and Van Dijk (1978), that provide guidance in how to best teach students to summarize their reading. These rules are as follows:

1. Don't include unnecessary, trivial, or repetitious details in the summary.

2. Collapse lists, such as of examples, details, actions, or traits. Students should be encouraged to provide a key word or phrase for the collapsed lists. For example, if the list contains the words *candy cane, wreath, present, mistletoe, reindeer,* and *Santa,* the key phrase might be *Christmas item.*

3. Utilize topic sentences to help frame the summary; if no topic sentence exists, the student must create one.

4. Integrate the information read by combining key words, key phrases, and existing and created topic sentences.

5. Once the summary is complete, revise or polish it, so it flows naturally as it is read. As Vacca and Vacca (2008) note, the process of revising the summary will cement its main points in the student's memory.

An effective summarizing strategy that supports Vacca and Vacca's guidelines for summary writing is Magnet Summaries (Buehl, 2001). In this strategy, students identify key words from the passages read and then use them to develop a summary of the passage. Furthermore, since this strategy asks students to chunk their reading into small sections and summarize each before developing a full-blown summary of the entire assignment, it is an excellent way to begin the task of teaching students to summarize.

Steps for a Magnet Summary

1. Students read a passage, usually the text developed under a single subheading section, and then determine a key word from the passage that relates directly to the concept being discussed.

2. Clarify for students that this key word is like a magnet in that it attracts information that is important to the topic.

3. Next, students recall all the details from the passage that are connected to the magnet word and record these on an index card.

4. After recording the magnet word and the supporting details on the index cards, students should develop the information into a short summary. Since this strategy focuses on relatively short reading passages such as those presented under a single subheading, strive to have students develop a one- to three-sentence summary whenever possible.

5. After students have summarized one section of the text, they should repeat the process until they have summarized all sections assigned.

6. Once all the sections have been summarized, ask students to arrange their sentences in logical order to develop a coherent summary for the entire reading assignment. Remind students that they may have to edit sentences so their summaries will flow smoothly.

The greatest advantage of teaching students how to summarize using the Magnet Summary strategy is that it provides them with a logical and simple procedure for determining relevant and irrelevant details as they synthesize the information. While this strategy appears simple, its success depends on teacher modeling to guide students through the process before they produce Magnet Summaries independently. See Figure 3.8 for an example of a Magnet Summary for science, Figure 3.9 for an example for mathematics, and Figure 3.21 for a reproducible master to use with the strategy.

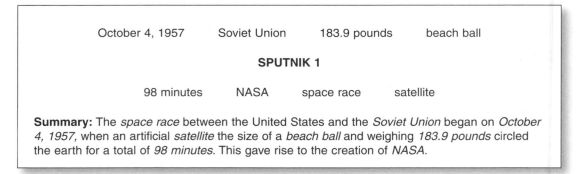

Figure 3.8 Example of Magnet Summary for Science

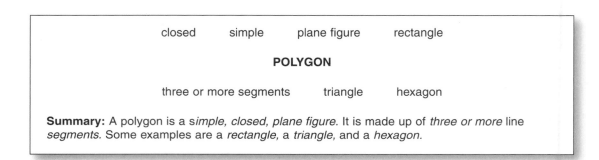

Figure 3.9 Example of Magnet Summary for Mathematics

Summary Graph

Students often have difficulty remembering what they read. This strategy helps students focus on the main ideas in each paragraph and requires students to write a sentence or two that synthesizes their ideas. Be sure to choose a short text like a biographical article, an introduction, summary of a chapter, or a short article.

Steps for a Summary Graph

1. Choose a text that has no more than five or six paragraphs. Create a graph that has the same number of columns as the text has paragraphs.

2. Tell the students to read one paragraph and to record the most important ideas from this paragraph in the first column of the graph.

3. Repeat the process until all of the paragraphs are read, and the graph is complete.

4. Students next reread the ideas in the graph and select one or two ideas from each column.

5. Then ask the students to use the ideas from the graph to write one or two complete sentences.

An example of a summary graph can be found in Figure 3.10.

Oscar Wilde (1854–1900)			
1	*2*	*3*	*4*
• Born in Ireland • An outstanding student of classical literature who traveled the world • A champion for the cause of aestheticism; motto "art for art's sake"	• Lived a Bohemian life in Paris • Wrote fairy tales, essays, and reviews • Published his most famous novel, *The Picture of Dorian Gray*	• Returned to the theater to support himself • Wrote four plays that were witty and satirical	• Sentenced to prison for immoral conduct • Deserted by his friends and died alone in Paris

Oscar Wilde was an Irish poet whose motto was "art for art's sake." Although he was a well-known author who wrote fairy tales, essays, reviews, *The Picture of Dorian Gray,* and four witty plays, he was imprisoned for immoral conduct and died penniless and alone.

Figure 3.10   Example of Summary Graph for English

Pyramid Diagram

Another strategy that helps students determine important details from their reading is the Pyramid Diagram (Solon, 1980, as found in Buehl, 2001). This strategy asks students to search out important facts and then, from those facts, draw conclusions and develop a summary of what was read.

Steps for a Pyramid Diagram

1. Develop a focusing question for students to use as they read the assigned material.

2. Instruct students that, as they read, they should record information pertinent to the focusing question on index cards. Encourage them to place only one fact on each index card. These cards will become Layer 4 in the Pyramid Diagram.

3. When students have completed the reading, place them in pairs or small groups, and instruct them to study all their cards and brainstorm possible categories under which the facts could be organized. (This is similar to the Open Sort strategy discussed in Chapter 2 of this text.) Once students have determined the categories they wish to use, instruct them to write each category title on an index card. These cards will become Layer 3 in the Pyramid Diagram.

Focusing Question: What causes led to the beginning of World War I?

	Causes of World War I	

World War I was caused by a combination of economic and political factors that were confounded by the creation of two major divisions of allies and fueled by a local conflict between two countries.

Economic Factors		*Political Factors*		*Allies*		*Local Conflict*	
New nations seek trade options.	New nations seek markets for goods.	New and old countries sought to be independent.	New nations built up power.	Old nations perceived build-up as threat.	Serbia, with Russian support, wanted to unite with Serbs in Austro-Hungarian Empire.	Austria, with German support, opposed Serbia's annexing attempts.	Archduke Ferdinand assassinated by Serb with military connections.	Britain, France, and Russia were one faction.	Austria, Hungary, and Germany were another faction.	Russia, Britain, and France joined forces against Austria, Hungary, and Germany to start war.
New nations become industrialized.										

Figure 3.11   Example of Pyramid Diagram for Social Studies

58

4. Next, students should arrange their fact cards under the appropriate category card.

5. When all the facts have been appropriately categorized, ask students to develop a title for the pyramid that reflects the overall topic. This card will become Layer 1 in the Pyramid Diagram.

6. Next, using all the information in the Pyramid Diagram, instruct students to write a brief summary of what they have learned on an index card, and place this card atop the category level. These cards will become Layer 2 in the Pyramid Diagram.

7. Finally, utilizing the entire Pyramid Diagram, students develop a full-paragraph conclusion relating to the focusing question by using Layer 2 of the pyramid as the topic sentence, items in Layer 3 to expand on the topic sentence, and items in Layer 4 to supply details to illustrate the points made.

See Figure 3.11 for an example of a Pyramid Diagram for social studies and Figure 3.22 for a reproducible master to use with this strategy.

Study Guide Strategies

Wood, Lapp, and Flood (1992) posit that asking students to read an entire chapter or book without some sort of assistance is an arduous assignment. Thus, in order to facilitate student learning, study guides have been developed to assist students as they read. Vacca and Vacca (2008) stress that effective study guides not only give students instructional support but foster their higher-order thinking skills as well. The following section describes a variety of study guides that can be developed to help students successfully comprehend their reading assignments.

Three-Level Guide

The Three-Level Guide (Herber, 1978) is similar to Raphael, Au, and Highfield's QAR strategy (2006) presented in the section on questioning earlier in this chapter. Once students understand how the QAR strategy works and understand that questions are classified by either being textually explicit or textually implicit, they are ready to utilize the Three-Level Guide strategy, which is based upon the same type of questioning. The QAR strategy's "right there" or textually explicit question corresponds to Herber's literal level, while the QAR strategy's "think and search" or textually implicit question corresponds to Herber's inferential level, and the QAR strategy's "author and you" and "on your own" questions correspond to Herber's application level.

The Three-Level Guide fosters students' ability to gather important information; ferret out the author's intended meaning by reading between the lines, making inferences, and drawing conclusions; and, finally, to apply what they have read to new and different life situations.

Steps for a Three-Level Guide

1. Identify specific ideas and concepts that reflect the author's intended and inferred meaning that you believe students should learn from the assignment.

2. From these ideas and concepts, develop five to six questions about these ideas and concepts; these become Level 2, the inferential level, of your guide.

3. Next, examine the questions you developed for Level 2 and determine what explicit facts are needed to support them. Questions to identify these facts are the items for Level 1 of the study guide. There should be at least two literal statements to support each major inference.

4. To develop Level 3, the applied level, construct four to five questions that ask students to make connections between what they already know (their prior knowledge) and what they have learned, and then ask them to apply their new knowledge.

5. Finally, to keep students focused and thinking, Vacca and Vacca (2008) suggest the addition of distracters or misleading facts to Levels 1 and 2; this, they say, discourages students from marking items indiscriminately.

As always, to assure proper scaffolding of this strategy, the teacher should model the strategy as a whole-class activity so students can later apply it independently. Figure 3.12 shows how the Three-Level Guide can be used with music appreciation; Figure 3.13 shows how it can be used with language arts/English.

Level 1

1. In what year was Richard Wagner born?

2. How many operas did Wagner compose?

Level 2

1. During the 19th and 20th centuries several major trends of thought saturated Germany. Which ones did Wagner embrace?

2. After reading the quotations about Wagner interspersed throughout the text, what political ideas did he embrace?

Level 3

1. We know that Richard Wagner inspired many musicians, but what other professions might he have inspired?

2. After studying the life, times, beliefs, and accomplishments of Wagner, what other creative being, past or present, do you think he can be compared to?

Figure 3.12 Example of Three-Level Guide for Music Appreciation

Level 1. Directions: Answer the following questions:

1. Who is Calpurnia?

2. What is her place in the Finch household?

Level 2. Directions: Check those statements that you feel represent the author's intended meaning.

1. Jem is beginning to understand more than Scout about Boo Radley.

2. Atticus Finch and Boo Radley were both very brave in this novel.

Level 3. Directions: What can we take from this reading as being important in our own lives? Read the following questions and respond.

1. In this novel Atticus tries to explain what he thinks real bravery is. Think of real world examples of both famous people and those who are less well known, choose someone who you think is brave, and explain why you think this person is brave.

2. Atticus Finch tells his children, "We were licked a hundred years before we started." If you had children today, how could you relate this statement to today's world?

Figure 3.13   Example of Three-Level Guide for Language Arts/English: *To Kill a Mockingbird*

Expository Text Structure Guide

In Chapter 1 we discuss the importance of teaching students to utilize text structures to help comprehend their content area textbooks. According to Roe et al. (2007), students who can recognize that a text follows a specific organizational pattern, such as cause-effect, problem-solution, comparison-contrast, definition-example, proposition-support, or sequential listing will be more skillful at comprehending what they read. The Structured Notetaking strategy discussed in Chapter 1 utilizes graphic organizers to help students identify patterns and, thus, locate the important ideas presented. A strategy similar to Structured Notetaking is the Expository Text Structure Guide (Tama & McClain, 2001), which uses an expository text format rather than a graphic organizer to illustrate the text pattern used. For an example of the Expository Text Structure Guide for science, see Figure 3.14, and for an example of how it might be used in social studies, see Figure 3.15.

Compare a Fixed Pulley . . .	To a Movable Pulley
1. The wheel moves, but the pulley does not move.	1. The pulley is attached to the load.
2. The pulley is attached to a bar or beam or other solid elevated position.	2. One end of the rope is attached to a fixed surface above the load.
3. The system has no mechanical advantage.	3. When the rope is pulled, the load moves.
4. The distance the force is applied is equal to the effort required to move the load.	4. The system does not change direction of effort.
5. The system can change the direction of effort.	5. The system has a mechanical advantage.
	6. The system reduces the effort needed to lift a load by half, so effort is gained.
	7. Distance is lost.

Figure 3.14   Example of Comparison-Contrast Expository Text Structure Guide for Science

Cause	Effect
Because: The British imposed the Tax Act and the Townshend Act. British soldiers harassed the colonists day and night. Colonists were confined to their homes by the British.	The colonists sought independence from Britain.

Figure 3.15   Example of Cause-Effect Expository Text Structure Guide for Social Studies

Point of View Study Guide

Another effective study guide is the Point of View Study Guide (Wood, 1988), which asks students to assume a role as they read the text. This allows students to gain a different perspective on the reading topic while they enhance their ability to recall and comprehend the information read. In addition, it encourages them to elaborate on the topic by utilizing their prior knowledge. It allows students to put newly acquired information into their own words while learning the content of the selection (Wood et al., 1992). This strategy follows an interview format, encouraging students to answer the interview questions in their own words but from the perspective of their assumed roles.

Steps for a Point of View Study Guide

1. Introduce a topic to students, and assign the accompanying reading.

2. After students have read the material, ask them to brainstorm the various perspectives from which the material could be read. For example, in reading a selection on global warming, students could assume the following perspectives: a weather forecaster, a farmer, an environmentalist, a specific animal such as a polar bear or a seal, a marine biologist, a zoologist, a government official, or an activist.

3. Next, for each perspective, create a series of interview questions that focus on the major content information in the selection from that perspective.

4. Students then choose or are assigned a specific perspective and reread material to answer the interview questions.

5. When students are ready to answer the interview questions, they present their information to the class in a dialogue format. Encourage them to elaborate with information from their personal experience as they present their interview to the class.

The Point of View Study Guide strategy allows students to become personally involved in their reading, thus making it an engaging activity. See Figure 3.16 to see how the Point of View Study Guide can be used for science and see how it is used for social studies in Figure 3.17.

Loons: The Voice of the Wilderness

Directions: You are about to be interviewed as if you were a male loon. As you read, answer the questions below as if you were a male loon.

1. What kind of loon are you?
2. What do you look like?
3. Does your mate look different? Explain.
4. Tell me about your bone structure.
5. What do you eat?
6. Are you a better swimmer and diver than walker? Why?
7. Why are you sitting on the nest?
8. How many babies do you usually have?
9. What kind of help will your baby need when it hatches?
10. What prevents you from having more babies?

Figure 3.16   Example of Point of View Study Guide for Science

---

Daily Life in Feudal England

Directions: You are about to be interviewed as if you were living in England during the Middle Ages. As you read, answer the questions below as if you were one of the following: (1) a lord, (2) a vassal, (3) a peasant, or (4) a serf. Then, in your group, prepare a presentation to share what your life is like.

   1. Describe where you live.

   2. Describe the kind of clothes you wear.

   3. What does a typical day in your life look like?

   4. What sort of jobs do you do?

   5. What responsibilities do you have?

   6. What types of people live around you?

   7. What dangers do you face?

   8. What good things do you experience?

   9. Explain how well you like living where you do.

  10. If you could choose to change anything in your life, what would you change and why?

Figure 3.17   Example of Point of View Study Guide for Social Studies

Critical Response Strategies

As teachers we all want our students to become critical thinkers. Roe et al. (2007) provide a clear profile of a critical thinker. In effect, these people are open-minded and avoid making judgments until they have verified all the facts. They constantly question the content they are studying and face the task with a problem-solving attitude. They evaluate the material they read for its content and its validity, such as its use of logic, propaganda, and language, as well as for the author's qualifications and purpose for writing. Tama and McClain (2001) remind us that critical thinking does not just magically appear in our students. They must be taught, "carefully taught," as the popular song from the musical *South Pacific* tells us. Tama and McClain (2001) also report that at Central Park East Secondary School in East Harlem, New York, students are encouraged to use their critical thinking skills every day, as they view the following questions posted in their classrooms:

- Whose voice am I hearing? From where is the statement or image coming?
- What is the point of view?

- What is the evidence? How do we know the speaker knows? How credible is the evidence?

- How do things fit together? What else do I know that fits this?

- What if? Could it be otherwise?

- What difference does it make? Who cares? Why should I care? (Tama & McClain, 2001, p. 112)

The following strategies foster critical thinking in students.

Critical Thinking Map

As noted above, students need to learn to be critical readers and thinkers. The Critical Thinking Map (Tama and McClain, 2001) asks students to move through a series of four steps as they (1) examine the main idea of a reading selection, (2) respond to what they have read by offering their own viewpoints and opinions as well as any other information or opinions that would apply to the reading, (3) draw their own conclusion from the reading by integrating what they have learned from the reading with their own prior knowledge as well as deciding whether the author's conclusions are valid, and (4) determine how what they have read can be relevant to issues in the world today.

Steps for a Critical Thinking Map

1. Show students the Critical Thinking Map graphic organizer and carefully explain each component. The components are as follows: Main Idea, Viewpoints and Opinions, Reader's Conclusions, Relevance to Today.

2. Model the strategy by reading a text segment aloud, and, after discussing each component, have students fill in the appropriate section of the graphic organizer.

3. Once students understand the process, allow them to work in small groups to complete a Critical Thinking Map. Be sure to allow time for students to discuss their responses and to check their work. Clarify all discrepant answers.

4. Finally, as soon as students can comfortably complete the strategy with few or no errors, encourage them to make use of the strategy independently.

See Figure 3.18 for an example of a Critical Thinking Map for social studies and Figure 3.23 for a reproducible master for the strategy.

After reading the assigned section of the text, complete the following Critical Thinking Map

Text _____ **Chapter** _____ **Section** _____ **Pages** _____

List the events, points, or steps that occurred in the section you read.
In 1820, Speaker of the House Henry Clay proposed the Missouri Compromise, which would admit Missouri as a slave state. All states south of the southern border of Missouri would be admitted to the Union as slave states, while states north of this border would be admitted as free states.
Summarize the main idea or message conveyed by the author in the section you read.
The Missouri Compromise allowed for an equal number of slave and free states, so the North and the South would stop their arguing.
Present viewpoints or opinions you hold about the section you read.
The compromise was designed to help settle an ugly problem, but it really did not focus on the real problem, making human beings slaves.
What conclusions did you reach about the section you read? Were the author's conclusions valid or invalid? Explain.
Henry Clay tried his best to handle a situation that he knew was serious and could escalate into a terrible war. Unfortunately, his solution was simply too simplistic to handle the situation. Perhaps he failed to have enough foresight to understand the real problem, or perhaps he was just looking for a quick fix. It did not work!
How is what you read in this section relevant to the world of today?
Through an understanding of the Missouri Compromise, we can see how a quick fix to a problem never works. It also makes us realize that we need to look at all aspects of a problem before we craft a solution to it.

Figure 3.18   Critical Thinking Map for Social Studies

REAP

Read-Encode-Annotate-Ponder is a teaching method developed by Eanet and Manzo (1976). This after-reading strategy helps students check for understanding and clarify and synthesize their thinking; it is intended to improve their comprehension, thinking, and writing skills.

Steps for REAP

Follow the four-step strategy symbolized by its title:

R = READ to discover the author's ideas.

E = ENCODE the author's ideas into one's own words.

A = ANNOTATE the ideas in writing from several perspectives.

P = PONDER what you have read and written; reflect on the meaning; seek connections.

While encoding or retelling helps students process what they read, annotation encourages students to construct deeper meaning of the text, thus promoting higher-level thinking skills. By definition, annotations are brief; they require more thinking than writing; however, it is active response that makes the ideas meaningful (Rosenblatt, 1994). An annotation can describe the basic ideas in the text or can go beyond the author's ideas to form personal applications and connections. You can introduce annotation types singly or a few at a time; however, they should encourage students to move beyond their initial response to perceive further meaning (Eanet & Manzo, 1976). See Figure 3.19 for an example of the REAP strategy for social studies. It includes a reading passage and examples of REAP annotation types to show how each step of the strategy can be used.

After students write their annotations, they can work alone, with a partner, or with a small group to ponder or reflect on the significance of the passage and their writing. They can share their ideas with the whole class. According to Fogarty (2002), much of the initial learning may be lost without this reflection. The reflective process is critical for transferring meaning.

REAP is a flexible strategy that can be used in a number of ways, particularly with technology. As students become more skilled in using this method, they can use annotations to respond to nontext experiences: a laboratory experiment, a piece of art or music, or another learning experience.

Selection to be read:

Segregation in South Africa

In 1948, the white government of South Africa passed laws to ensure that whites would retain control of the country. Those laws established a system of apartheid, which divided South Africans into four segregated racial groups—whites, blacks, mixed races, and Asians. The system limited the jobs nonwhites could hold, controlled where they could live, and restricted their rights. Because of apartheid, the black African majority were also denied the right to vote.

Annotation Types and Examples

1. **Short Response: briefly states the main ideas or themes in the passage**

   In 1948, the white government of South Africa created the system of apartheid, which placed strict limitations on all nonwhites.

2. **Question: creates a question based on the main points in the text**

   How did the government in South Africa help its white citizens maintain power?

3. **Critical: states the author's view and states whether the reader agrees or disagrees with the view**

   The leaders of the white government in South Africa felt threatened by the black African majority in their country. They needed to realize that discrimination of any type is wrong.

4. **Comparison/Contrast: identifies the ideas in the text and relates them to similar or different ideas**

   The laws that created the apartheid system in South Africa remind me of Rosa Park's bus boycott, which protested discrimination in the South.

5. **Creative: makes connections and suggests different views and applications to learning**

   The desire to have power over others often makes leaders pass laws that do not consider the good of all people.

Figure 3.19 Example of REAP Strategy

Reader Response

Many trace the beginning of the reader response theory to Louise Rosenblatt's classical work, *Literature as Exploration* (1938). Rosenblatt's reader response theory has served as a model for teaching literary texts and emphasizes the importance of the reader's role in interpreting texts. Students learn to create their own meaning or interpret the significance of a text themselves rather than relying on a teacher or critic to give an analysis.

Various responses to literature have been utilized since Rosenblatt's (1938) culminating work. Bleich's (1978) method of encouraging expressive interpretation is a unique way to get students to respond to a text. Students are requested to think about their responses to the text in two different ways—affectively and associatively—and write their responses in a journal or notebook.

Teachers can use some of the following questions as a guide in eliciting a response to reading from their students:

1. How did this piece affect you?
2. Why did this piece affect you in this way?
3. What experiences did you think about as you read the text?
4. What is the most important idea, word, line, or scene in the text? Why do you believe it is important?
5. How does this piece remind you of other literary works?

To use this strategy effectively, encourage students to develop their ideas and thoughts into material that is valuable for others. Then ask them share their responses with small groups or with the whole class. In this way, students learn how to communicate their ideas with others, so they can move beyond their own experiences and think about different meanings of the text. Students in reader-response classrooms become active learners. Bleich's method encourages students to respond to the text in different ways, thus developing their creative and critical thinking skills. Because their responses are valued, they feel empowered to make judgments about what they read.

Point, Counterpoint Strategy

The Point, Counterpoint strategy was developed by Rogers (1990) as a way of helping students develop their own interpretation of stories rather than depend on conventional explanations or rely on the teacher's viewpoint. According to Rogers, students need to have practice in dealing with the intricacies of complex narratives. They must learn how to interpret textual information and to utilize extratextual resources to derive their own meaning.

Steps for the Point, Counterpoint Strategy

This strategy consists of three stages:

1. Initial responses to the story
2. Discussion of responses
3. Development of final responses

Stage 1: Initial responses to the story

As students read, they keep individual notes about anything that comes to mind to help them understand and interpret the text. For example, they can use ideas related to characters, setting, or plot; personal connections; or questions about the text. Upon completion of the initial reading and note taking, students review their notes and take 10 minutes to answer the following prompts:

1. Identify a significant theme.

2. Which ideas in the selection are related to the theme?

3. How do the ideas connect to your knowledge or experiences?

Stage 2: Discussion of responses

At this stage, students share their responses with the class and are encouraged to listen to other interpretive and critical viewpoints. Students need to be prepared to defend their views and yet be open-minded enough to understand that there can be a variety of critical interpretations. The teacher's task is to act as a facilitator for the discussion and to jot down essential discussion points as needed.

Stage 3: Development of final responses

This stage allows students to develop their initial responses to the text by revising them. Ideally, their responses take the form of self-assessment, so they include some of their ideas and incorporate others' viewpoints. Students will schedule conferences with the teacher for assistance.

The Point, Counterpoint Reading strategy provides teachers with a framework to expose students to different interpretations of literature and to engage in a discussion of contrasting viewpoints, and it encourages students to reflect on, assess, and revise their original interpretations.

Rogers developed the Point, Counterpoint strategy for use with advanced high school students; however, the strategy lends itself to a number of adaptations, including responding to the selection with sketches (Harste, Short, & Burke, 1988); using a Venn diagram to compare and contrast viewpoints; engaging in a debate; and writing a group essay, skit, or dialogue.

CHAPTER SUMMARY

As discussed at the beginning of this chapter, there are specific processes that students must be able to complete and skills they must have in order to successfully comprehend both the narrative and expository texts they are required to read in the various content area disciplines they study. In addition, those content area disciplines present certain comprehension challenges as well. To help students learn more effectively, this chapter provides a variety of learning strategies that can be used in all content area disciplines.

DISCUSSION CUBE

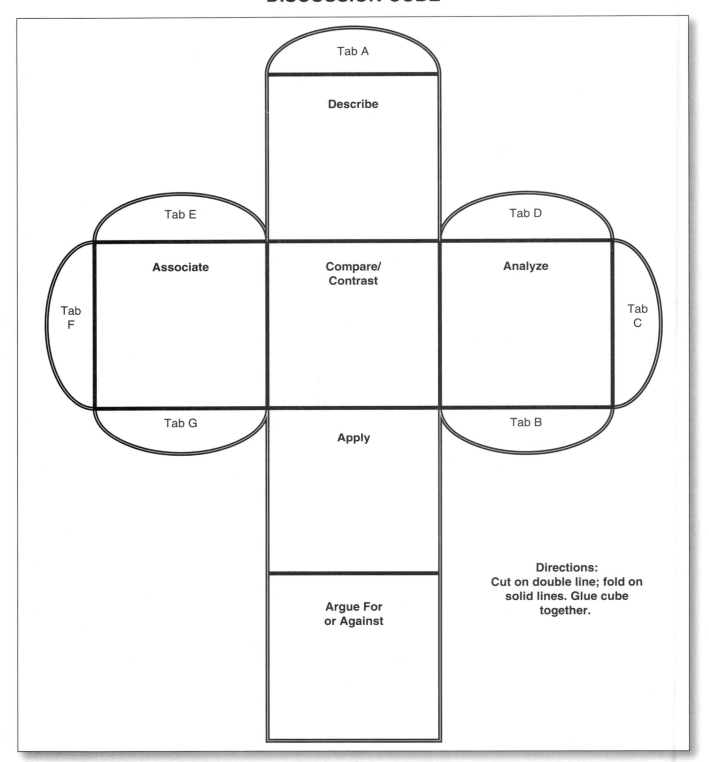

Figure 3.20 Reproducible Master for a Discussion Cube

SOURCE: Cube form adapted from R. G. Meyer and Southern Regional ETTC.

MAGNET SUMMARY

KEYWORDS

_____   _____   _____

MAGNET WORD

KEYWORDS

_____   _____   _____

SUMMARY

Figure 3.21   Reproducible Master for Magnet Summary

SOURCE: From *Reading and Writing Across Content Areas* (2nd ed., p. 177), by R. L. Sejnost and S. Thiese, 2007, Thousand Oaks, CA: Corwin. Copyright © 2007 by Corwin. Reprinted with permission.

PYRAMID DIAGRAM

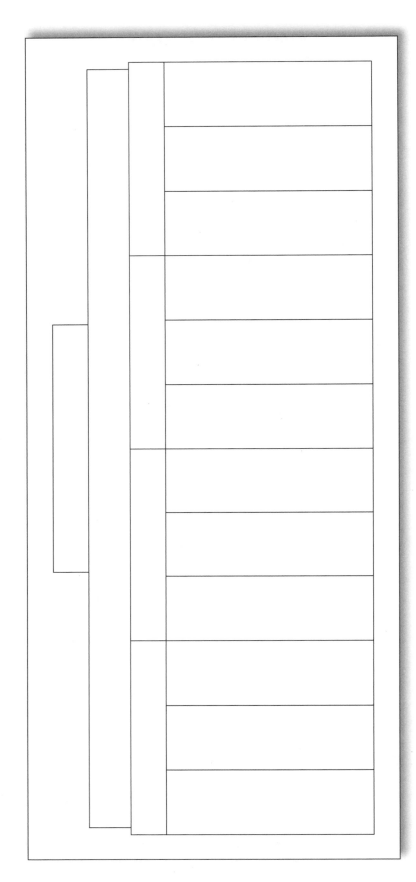

Figure 3.22   Reproducible Master for a Pyramid Diagram

CRITICAL THINKING MAP

After reading the assigned section of the text, complete the following Critical Thinking Map.

Text _____   **Chapter** _____   **Section** _____   **Pages** _____

List the events, points, or steps that occurred in the section you read.
Summarize the main idea or message conveyed by the author in the section you read.
Present viewpoints or opinions you hold about the section you read.
What conclusions did you reach about the section you read? Were the author's conclusions valid or invalid? Explain.
How is what you read in this section relevant to the world of today?

Figure 3.23   Reproducible Master of a Critical Thinking Map

CHAPTER 4

Writing to Learn in Content Area Disciplines

Reading usually precedes writing and the impulse to write is almost always fired by reading. Reading, the love of reading, is what makes you dream of becoming a writer.

Susan Sontag

A RATIONALE FOR WRITING TO LEARN

As teachers, we are well aware of the phenomenon that we often see: The students who are good readers are often the good writers as well. Vacca and Vacca (2008) suggest that since good readers tend to read more, they are, as a result, exposed to more writing, which helps them to become better writers. And, since they are both good readers and good writers, they are simply willing to read and write more, giving truth to the adage "practice makes perfect." Whatever the reason, the fact remains: There does seem to be a connection between reading and writing.

Roe, Stoodt-Hill, and Burns (2007) remind us that both reading and writing are sources of communication that involve the use of written language skills. In addition, they seem to complement one another, since one must have access to written material for reading to occur, and of what use is written material unless someone reads it? Furthermore, Tierney and Pearson (1983), Vacca and Vacca (2008), and Raphael and Englert (1990) clarify that reading and writing are acts of composition, and both require the process of constructing meaning. As Vacca and Vacca (2008) note, "Whereas the writer works to make text sensible, the reader works to make sense from a text" (p. 246). Furthermore, Vacca and Vacca (2008) tell us that the processes of reading and writing share certain characteristics, since both "involve purpose, commitment, schema activation, planning, working with ideas, revision and rethinking, and monitoring" (p. 246).

Since such an obvious connection exists between reading and writing, it is no wonder that educators are anxious to develop this connection in their classrooms. According to Konopak, Martin, and Martin (1987) and Shanahan (1990), when reading and writing activities are combined, student achievement increases. This is especially true in the content area classroom, where the basic format is the learning and retention of the facts, concepts, and ideas of specific disciplines. In essence, in order to successfully learn in a variety of content area disciplines, students must not only possess the ability to ferret out information at the literal level, they must also be able to process that information critically, thus engaging their higher-order thinking skills. And according to several studies, writing promotes the critical thinking and learning skills needed to efficiently achieve in any content area discipline (Britton, Burgess, Martin, McLeod, & Rosen, 1975; Emig, 1977; Herrington, 1981; Knoblauch & Brannon, 1983; Odell, 1980; Parker, 1985). Furthermore, Emig suggests that "writing, in fact, represents a unique mode of learning—not merely valuable, not merely special, but unique" (p. 122), because, according to Emig, Fulwiler (1982), and Tomlinson (1990), it places the new knowledge learned into a cognitive framework, thus providing a process by which this new knowledge is connected to prior knowledge and experience. The final result, then, is a concrete, visible product that exhibits what has been learned.

In effect, then, writing can not only be a means of evaluating what a student knows and understands about a topic of study, it can also engage students in the actual act of learning the topic itself; this kind of writing is known as *writing to learn,* for it enables students to process and organize their thoughts and ideas about what they are studying as well as formulate and extend their thinking about it. It strengthens and crystallizes the process of making meaning. In fact, the research of Langer and Applebee (1987) indicates that writing is a meaning-making process that facilitates the learner's ability to make predications, build connections, raise questions, discover new ideas, and promote higher-level thinking. These thoughts are further supported by Forsman (1985), who reminds us that, as educators, we can either sentence our students to mindless mechanical operations or facilitate their ability to think; writing, she states, is one of the most effective ways to develop thinking.

In addition, many writing activities provide overlapping purposes; for example, writing about an experiment in a science class gives students practice in recording observable data and questions that come to mind and, at the same time, engages them in valuable science writing. The key to using activities like these effectively, researchers contend, lies in matching the activity with the learning situation. Different types of assignments may be more valuable than others in diverse contexts (Bangert-Drowns, Hurley, & Wilkinson, 2004; Cantrell, Fusaro, & Dougherty, 2000). And, as with any other type of assignment, teachers should think carefully about how well a task corresponds with learning objectives, with students' needs and abilities, and with the way students will be assessed (Barr & Healy, 1988). Furthermore, in a meta-analysis of 48 research studies, of students at elementary through college levels, that examined relationships between classroom writing-to-learn activities and student achievement on writing to learn, Bangert-Drowns et al. discovered that writing to learn is much more than simple writing instruction. Based on their analysis, the researchers concluded that writing-to-learn activities produced a positive impact on academic achievement, especially when the writing-to-learn activities were repeated over long periods of time. Thus, it is apparent that while the vehicle of writing to learn asks students to write more and to write better, its real value lies in the fact that when students write to learn, they integrate their writing strategies with the concepts learned in their content area classes. It is this strategic integration that leads to authentic learning, because as Mitchell (1996) reminds us, when students write to learn, they must not only think about what they have read but also find the words to explain what they have learned and how they understand that learning as well as how they have processed that learning.

WRITING-TO-LEARN STRATEGIES

Learning Logs and Journals

Probably the best known of the writing-to-learn strategies, learning logs and journals ask students to explore course content in writing. Assignments are typically short and informal and can be performed either in or out of class.

Learning Logs

Learning logs typically focus on work that students are doing in the classroom and generally do not include comments about personal matters. They often involve the use of a prompt related to material that has been covered or an activity experienced in class (Christenbury, 2006). The common purpose is to have students make entries in their logs during the first or last five minutes of class or after each completed week of class. Logs can include problem-solving entries from mathematics or science, observations from lab experiments, questions about lectures or readings, lists of books students have read or would like to read, and homework assignments. They are beneficial for teachers as well as students, because they can give teachers insights into students' development. The following prompts can be used to help students in making thoughtful entries in their learning logs:

1. Write three sentences describing what you learned today.

2. List five things that you did in class today.

3. Write three questions that you have about what we did in class today.

4. Explain how something you learned today connects to another lesson.

5. Write the most important idea from today's lessons.

6. Write three questions that might be on the test.

7. Write an explanation to another student of what you learned.

8. Reread yesterday's learning log; rewrite that entry in another format.

9. What was the most interesting thing you learned today? Why?

10. What confused you about this lesson?

Journals

A journal is a personal record of experiences and reflections. People keep journals for a variety of reasons. Professional and amateur writers use journals to record their thoughts, generate ideas for future writing, and experiment with language. Scientists and social scientists record the observations from their fieldwork in logs or notebooks. Many professionals, including teachers and librarians, keep journals during internships or independent study projects to record and reflect upon their professional growth.

Teachers find that using journals is valuable, because journals encourage students to convey their ideas and thoughts about the content, apply the lessons to actual situations, express their views about issues, make their learning personal, and improve thinking and writing (Fulwiler, 1987). In general, teachers in all content areas have discovered that when students write about course readings, lectures, and discussions, they understand what they know and do not know about a lesson and how the information relates to them.

Journals come in many forms, and teachers should choose their own way of using them in the classroom. Some teachers like to use prompts, because the prompts help students focus on the content and convey their feelings about the subject matter. The following prompts can be used to help students in making thoughtful entries in their journals:

1. What aspects of colonial life seemed most difficult?

2. Which features of technological change were innovative?

3. Why was there such diversity of opinion during the end of the Romantic era?

4. Which discovery is most beneficial for our lives?

5. What major differences did you see between the two [characters, scientists, inventors] as to their [points of view, ideologies, ways to solve problems]?

6. What aspects of the [author's, researcher's] life are evident in [his, her] work?

7. Explain how the reading connects to your life.

8. Make a map of the [steps of an experiment, explorer's journey, character's journey]. Document what happens in each phase. Explain which part was the most difficult.

Double-Entry Journals

Double-entry journals offer students a way to interact personally with the text by reflecting on and writing about their understanding of the material they are reading. Students can use these journals to convey their ideas, to express an opinion, and to make connections to the text, thus increasing reading comprehension (Vaughn, 1990).

Double-entry journals take different shapes and forms. Traditionally, the double-entry journal is a two-column journal.

Steps for the Double-Entry Journal

1. Direct students to read a section or sections of a text.

2. In the left column, students write information from the text, such as a quotation or concept they want to discuss, or a question. They should include the page number where they found the information.

3. In the right column, students respond to the information written in the left column by recording opinions, reactions, questions, analysis, and concerns.

See Figure 4.1 for an example of a double-entry journal for science.

Ideas From the Text: Frogs	Response
• Frogs use their ability to see at close range to detect their prey; however, the victim needs to move in order to set off the frog's feeding response. The prey is captured by means of the back end of the tongue, and the food is swallowed with little or no chewing. (54) • Frogs eat almost any creature that is not too small to be a waste of effort, including ants, wasps, spiders, fish, and other frogs. (55)	• I thought the frog sensed its prey, and I was surprised that it had to wait for the prey to move before it could eat the prey. • I knew that frogs ate flies but did not realize that they were willing to capture so many different kinds of animals.

Figure 4.1   Example of a Double-Entry Journal for Science

A popular variation to the double-entry journal asks students to respond to the text and make connections to the world and their lives. This method helps students make multiple interpretations and connections to the text, thus helping them to become better critical thinkers and readers. See Figure 4.2 for an example of a double-entry journal variation for English.

Quotation From the Text	Response
It was the yellow gulf weed that had made so much phosphorescence in the night. "Fish," he said, "I love you and respect you very much. But I will kill you dead before this day ends." (54)	Santiago is a very caring and sensitive person, despite the fact that he has to kill the fish. He know that he must return to shore with the dead fish, because he has had so many days of bad luck; however, the fish has almost become a part of him. He admires its persistence and seemingly undying strength. The beast keeps swimming, even with the weight of the rowboat connected to it. Santiago admires and respects his prey. **Connection to the world:** This passage relates to the candidates running in the Democratic primary. Hilary Clinton and Barack Obama both have the same dream in mind: to become president of the United States. Even though they are rivals, they respect one another in their views and standings. Ultimately, only one of them will be the victor. **Connection to my life:** When I read the passage, I thought about my participation in cross country and track. Whenever I race against others, I recognize their talents and abilities and respect them. However, when I get ready to race, I only think about my desire to win. I will do my best to defeat them before the end of the day.

Figure 4.2   Example of a Double-Entry Journal for *The Old Man and the Sea*

Extended Writing-to-Learn Strategies

As noted above, writing enables students to process, organize, formulate, and extend their thinking about what they have been learning. In addition, teachers can also assign writing to help students evaluate what they know and understand about a topic. The following writing-to-learn strategies help foster students' abilities to make predications, build connections, raise questions, discover new ideas, and promote higher-level thinking.

Shrinklit

The Shrinklit is a poetic form used to synthesize literature. Poetry has been used for years in many content areas to enhance curricula and assist in the learning of concepts, and when students use poetry to recall their thinking, they are more likely to remember it. The use of poetry clarifies concepts in ways that direct instructional methods cannot. Thus, writing a Shrinklit—a short, poetic summary of chapters or short pieces of literature—is an effective tool for learning (Sagoff, 1971).

Steps for the Shrinklit Strategy

1. Ask students to choose a few chapters in a novel or a short piece of literature.
2. Tell them to write a poem that focuses on the main ideas in the assigned piece of literature.
3. The poem should be at least 10 lines long.
4. They should use figurative language (alliteration, personification, similes, etc).
5. Students should share their ideas with a small group of students or with the class.

See Figure 4.3 for an example of a Shrinklit for English.

Great Expectations Chapters 1–4

Pip stands by the tombstones, reading the inscriptions.

Sad to be one of the few survivors in his family.

An old man startles him, threatens his life

All for some food and a file—

Pip sees the leg irons, knows he must obey.

Steals food from his sister—fearful of getting caught.

Soldiers come seeking help—looking for convicts.

Pip and Joe follow them; criminals are caught.

One confesses to the crime—Pip still feels guilty,

Worries he'll be punished—tickler again.

Figure 4.3 Example of a Shrinklit for English: *Great Expectations,* Chapters 1–4

Probable Passages

In Chapter 2, the vocabulary strategy Possible Sentences (Moore & Moore, 1986) was presented. Probable Passages (Wood, 1984) is a writing strategy that is very similar, since, like Possible Sentences, it is based upon snippets of actual texts that students use to predict the content of the passage from which the text has been snipped. Furthermore, much like the Possible Sentences strategy, Probable Passages encourages readers to make connections to what they already know (their prior knowledge), as well as to their own experiences, other texts they have read, and their knowledge of the world, to predict what ideas and concepts the text they are about to read might contain. In addition, similar to the Structured Notetaking procedure (Smith & Tompkins, 1988) discussed in Chapter 1, Probable Passages makes students aware of both the story structure found in narrative writing, and, as Readence, Bean, and Baldwin (2004) note, the text structures of cause-effect, comparison-contrast, and problem-solution seen in expository writing. Finally, this strategy is also similar to the Story Impressions strategy (Denner & McGinley, 1986) discussed in Chapter 2, since students utilize a list of vocabulary words to predict the content of what they are to read. Overall, however, the real power of the Probable Passages strategy is that it helps students scaffold their self-monitoring abilities, so they become aware of when their reading and writing fails to make sense, thus fostering both recall and comprehension. In order for this strategy to be successful, the teacher should model this strategy before students use it independently.

Steps for Probable Passages

1. To begin, prepare a list of vocabulary words that contains important concepts from the text and that represents the categories in either the narrative or expository text to be studied. For example, if the text is narrative, include words that reflect the characters, setting, problem, and outcomes, and if the text is expository, include words that relate to the specific text structure, such as cause-effect, comparison-contrast, and problem-solution.

2. Present the list to the students, and identify the specific text structure utilized. For clarity, students can be given a template that reflects the elements of the text's structure.

3. For narrative texts, students place each vocabulary word in the category (characters, setting, problem, or outcomes) where they feel it most likely belongs, and then they write a probable passage that reflects what they think the text might say.

4. For expository text, Readence et al. (2004) suggest that you choose one category of the text structure—such as the problem in the problem-solution structure, the comparison in the comparison-contrast structure, or the effect in the cause-effect structure—and ask students to do the following:

   a. First, develop a text frame that relates to the category, with blanks where the selected vocabulary words would fit. Students then fit the selected words into the text frame.

   b. Next, develop a second text frame that supplies a beginning sentence that foreshadows the second part of the text structure—such as the solution in the problem-solution structure, the contrast in the comparison-contrast structure, or the cause in the cause-effect structure—and ask students to attempt to write a probable passage.

5. In a final step, students read the selected narrative or expository text to determine if their predictions for both the text frame and probable passage were correct. Then they edit their original probable passage to include any missing information and correct anything that is wrong.

See Figure 4.4 for an example of a Probable Passage for science or social studies.

Brazil

Vocabulary Words for Important Concepts

Text Frame: **Cause**   **Effect**

                    trees   jungle
                    farmers   rare species
                    burn   trees
                    increase farm land   animals

Probable Passage:

Brazil's jungle and the animals in it are facing extinction. Sometimes farmers burn down jungles to increase farm land, and sometimes illegal logging projects cut down the trees. This all destroys the rare species of trees and animals in the Brazilian jungles.

Figure 4.4 Example of a Probable Passage for Science or Social Studies

Guided Writing Procedure

The Guided Writing Procedure (GWP) (Smith & Bean, 1980) is a strategy that is based on a three-day process that enhances comprehension by fostering the students' ability to synthesize and retain the content area material they have been studying. According to Smith and Bean, the Guided Writing Procedure is designed to

- activate and sample students' prior knowledge about a topic to be studied before they begin learning about it.
- sample and evaluate how well students can express their thoughts in writing in a specific content area discipline.
- improve the students' overall writing abilities through careful thought and revision.

While the GWP may seem to be time consuming, the research of Konopak et al. (1987) illustrates that if students use this strategy, the quality of their writing is greatly improved, because they are able to integrate their prior knowledge about the topic of study with what they learn from a text and then produce a carefully edited, readable piece of writing. This improvement in the students' writing is facilitated by the teacher's continual monitoring of that writing, which guides the students' editing and revision processes and eventually leads to a well-thought-out and developed piece of content area writing. In effect, "the GWP is an in-depth exploration of a text reading assignment" (Readence et al. 2004, p. 196), and this is an exploration we sincerely want our students to make.

Steps for the Guided Writing Procedure

Day 1:

1. Students brainstorm what they know about an upcoming topic of study and record their responses, including a list of terms relative to the topic.

2. After students have developed the list, instruct them to identify categories that encompass the brainstormed terms and list details that support their choices of categories.

3. Next, students incorporate the terms and details in an organized form, such as an outline, web, or graphic organizer.

4. Finally, using the outline, web, or graphic organizer as a guide and a rubric for good writing, students write a short paragraph depicting what they know about the topic. This is a first draft.

5. When students have completed their first drafts, collect them and evaluate them on the basis of good writing criteria. Readence et al. (2004) suggest that these criteria are topic, supporting details, logical flow, word choice, grammar, and mechanics. These criteria are best judged through the use of a rubric.

Note: During this first phase of the GWP, read the students' drafts, but do not make any discernible marks on the manuscripts.

Day 2:

1. Return the students' first drafts along with a copy of the rubric used to evaluate the drafts.

2. Using the evaluation rubric, students edit or revise their first drafts. The resulting papers become their second drafts.

3. Students turn in their second drafts and the original rubric for a second round of teacher evaluation.

4. At this point, give students a reading assignment related to the topic of study. Tell students that the purpose of the reading is to locate additional ideas, details, and examples to add to their writing.

Day 3:

1. As they did on Day 1, students need to record the new information garnered from their reading and add it to their original outlines, graphic organizers, or webs. (Note: Students may need help in this revision process as they add and delete information.)

2. Finally, armed with this new information, students develop their final drafts. This final draft now contains an integration of information from the students' prior knowledge as well as what was learned from the text, lectures, videos, etc. See Figure 4.5 for an example of the Guided Writing Procedure for science.

Topic: The Bald Eagle

Day 1:

Brainstorming

North America	Canada	Florida	California	swim
fly	dive	fish	small mammals	water birds

Outline

I. Habitat
   A. North America
   B. Canada
   C. Florida
   D. California

II. Habits
   A. swim
   B. fly
   C. dive

III. Diet
   A. fish
   B. small mammals
   C. water birds

Paragraph

The American eagle has a big habitat. It flies cross North America, Canada, Florida, and California. It swims and dives to catch fish, small mammals, and water birds.

Day 2: Revision of draft completed on Day 1

The American eagle has a large habitat range. It can be found across North America from Canada down to the United States and across Florida to the furthermost tips of California. As it flies, swims, and dives across its habitat, it hunts fish, small mammals, and water birds to exist.

Day 3: Paragraph written after reading information on the topic

The bald eagle, our national bird, has a large habitat range. It is unique to North America and can be found across North America from Alaska and Canada all the way down to northern parts of Mexico, including Baja California. Most bald eagles, 60%, in fact, are found in Alaska.

Since bald eagles usually live near woodlands and waterways such as the coastlines of lakes and rivers, they depend on hunting for small woodland mammals and fishing for fish and water birds. They can soar through the air at speeds that range between 20 and 40 miles per hour, and when they spot a fish, they can dive at speeds of over 100 miles per hour.

Figure 4.5   Example of a Guided Writing Procedure for Science

RAFT

RAFT, an acronym for **R**ole, **A**udience, **F**ormat, and **T**opic (Santa, 1988) is a popular writing strategy that fosters students' ability to think critically and reflect while they synthesize what they have learned. It also helps to strengthen their sense of what it means to be a writer by making them aware of the impact that the topic and the format can have on their audience. Furthermore, the RAFT strategy is effective, because it requires that students examine a topic they have studied from a perspective different from their own and then write about that topic for an audience they may not be familiar with in a format that may be new to them. For maximum success with the strategy, the teacher should model it before students use it independently.

Steps for RAFT

1. First introduce the elements of the RAFT strategy to the students.

    R = role of the writer (Who is the writer? What role does he or she play?)

    A = audience for the writer (To whom are you writing? Who will read your writing?)

    F = format of the writing (What form will your writing take?)

    T = topic of the writing (What will you be writing about?)

2. Next, together with the students, determine the important ideas, concepts, or information from the reading assignment in order to determine the topic of the assignment.

3. Then, with students, brainstorm possible roles class members could assume in their writing. This will determine the role for the assignment.

4. Now, ask students to determine the audience for this writing.

5. Finally, decide the format the writing will take.

Note: Until students become familiar with using the RAFT strategy, it is usually more effective to assign all students the same role, audience, format, and topic for their writing. Then, as students become familiar with the process, they should be allowed to brainstorm their own role, audience, and format. See Figure 4.6 for a list of suggested topics to use RAFT with and Figure 4.7 for an example of the RAFT strategy for science.

Role	Audience	Format	Topic
For Mathematics			
Polygon	Graphic artist	Set of instructions	Presenting attributes, abilities to be featured in an illustration
Algebraic equation	Parentheses	Love letter	What parentheses can do for equations
Journalist	Public	News release	Steps in solving a linear equation
Rational number	Another fraction	Letter	How fractions work together to produce a sum, difference, quotient, or product
For Science			
Environmentalist	Tourists	Informational flyer	Facts about the bald eagle
Water	Plants	Poem	How the sun helps plants grow
Advertiser	Television executive	Infomercial	How to prevent mosquito-borne diseases
Blood	The body	An essay	How the blood protects against infection
For Social Studies			
Lawyer	Student	Brief	Driving under the influence
Election judge	Voting citizens	Pamphlet	Importance and rules of voting
Cartoon journalist	Newspaper readers	Political cartoon	Current political issue
Lawyer	Jury	An opinion	Pros and cons of the death penalty
For English/Language Arts			
Robert Browning	Readers	An ode	Elizabeth Browning
Literary critic	Book review magazine	Criticism	The latest novel read
Advice columnist	Othello	Advice column	Desdemona's fidelity
Newspaper reporter	Residents of Maycomb	Obituary	Qualities of Boo Radley
For Other Subjects			
Judge	Teenage driver	Ruling	Driving under the influence
Diego Rivera	Frida Kahlo	Detailed explanation	Mural painting
Treble clef	Bass clef	Friendly letter	How they are different
Computer	Users	A flow chart	The components of a CPU

Figure 4.6 Suggested Topics for RAFT

ROLE = Environmentalist

AUDIENCE = Tourists

FORMAT = Informational Flyer

TOPIC = Facts About the Bald Eagle

Have You Seen Me? Protect Me!

Who: American Bald Eagle, the national bird of the United States

Where: Habitat ranges across Canada, Alaska, North America, and Northern Mexico

What: I live to be 30 to 40 years old.
I am a male, I weigh about 9 pounds.
If I am a female, I weigh about 13 pounds.
I have a wingspan of seven feet.
I fly from at speeds of 20 to 40 miles per hour.
I dive at speeds of over 100 miles per hour.
I live where woodlands and waterways abound.

Why: I am on the threatened species list.

No one can take, transport, sell, barter, trade, import, or export me or be in possession of any of my feathers or body parts.

Figure 4.7   Example of RAFT for Science

The Multigenre Report

The Multigenre Report is a creative approach that is guaranteed to motivate students to write to learn. First proposed by Romano (2000), the Multigenre Report is simply a collection of student written pieces of varying genres that depict a central theme or topic that students have studied about. The pieces they write can include a variety of compositions such as the following: narratives, expositions, poems, songs, raps, letters, memos, notes, diaries, journals, essays, lists, scripts, newspaper articles, editorials, advertisements, birth certificates or announcements, death certificates, obituaries, and even drawings. They can be of varying lengths as well. Moulton (1999), Allen (2001) and Grierson, Anson, and Baird (2002) all present variations of the Multigenre Report by suggesting that it can be utilized as a research project or an author study wherein students compose a collage of creative compositions that reflect what they have learned from researching a topic.

While Tama and McClain (2001) stress the value of using the Multigenre Report as a research project, they note that its open-ended nature may be disconcerting to students who need more structure. As a result, they suggest that teachers provide clear parameters and directions for their students, such as stipulating the number and types of genres to be included as well as the specific components to be developed, such as a table of contents, endnotes, and a bibliography. Figure 4.8 provides some ideas for a cross-curricular Multigenre Report for science, English, social studies, and consumer studies, based on an endangered species.

Encyclopedia Article

The Common Loon

Loons have stout bodies, long necks, pointed bills, and three-toed webbed feet. They spend most of their time afloat, since their heavy, low-slung bodies make movement on land slow and awkward. As a result, common loons spend little time on land and pull themselves onto land only to nest. They generally move one foot at a time to walk, shuffling along with their breasts close to the ground.

The summer plumage of the common loon is very striking with its black and white checkered back, glossy black head, characteristic white necklace around the throat, and bright red eyes. The white feathers of the belly and wing linings are present year-round, but all loons, young and adult, have grayish feathers in the winter. Both males and females sport the same plumage colorings, although males are generally larger. Loon adults are large bodied, weighing from 2.7 to over 6.3 kilograms and measuring almost a meter from bill tip to outstretched feet. Their bill, which is black in color, is quite large, averaging 75 mm in length.

The skeleton and muscular systems of a loon are designed for swimming and diving; their legs are placed far back on their bodies, which gives them excellent movement capabilities in water but makes them ungainly on land. Their heads can be held directly in line with their necks during diving to reduce drag, and their legs have powerful muscles for swimming. Many bones of the loon's body are solid, rather than hollow like those of other birds. These heavy bones make loons less buoyant and help them to dive. The loon's large webbed feet provide propulsion underwater, and their wings are used only for turning underwater.

Letter to the Editor

Dear Editor,

Each summer when I visit the lakes in your area, I have enjoyed the haunting voices of the loons calling across the lake in the early morning and at dusk. This year, however, I heard few of those calls, and I am deeply concerned about that. As a result, I contacted the Department of Wildlife to find out why there seemed to be so few loons in the area this year. And, I was horrified to learn that the common loon is in danger of disappearing from our waters.

According to the Department of Wildlife, even though all loons are protected by federal law, may not be hunted, and still nest in large numbers across Canada and the United States, recent studies have shown low breeding success. This is because the loon nests in populated areas, so it suffers the effects of pollution, development, and disturbance. Loss of breeding habitat from lakeshore development and spills of oil and other pollutants make safe breeding difficult. In addition, wakes caused by boats and water skiers often swamp or destroy nests or cause loons to abandon some nesting sites. Furthermore, increased lake acidity also affects the loons' survival, since acidity results in a decrease of fish and other foods, causing loon chicks on very acid lakes to starve. Acidification of lakes also increases the rate of methylmercury production in lake sediments and water, thus giving loons mercury poisoning or causing them to lay fewer eggs. Finally, careless fisherman also add to the problem, since their use of lead sinkers can lead to lead poisoning, which loons can get after eating fish with lead sinkers or picking up discarded sinkers from the lake bottom. And, abandoned or unattended fishing line and hooks also cause loon injury and death.

So, let's protect the loons we have left. To do this, boats should be kept away from swimming birds and chicks too young to dive or fly. Some shoreline areas should be left undisturbed so loons can nest, and boaters who pass should travel at low speed to prevent wakes. Anglers must use nonlead sinkers and be sure that no hooks or lines are left unattended or abandoned. We must strive to save the loon, the "voice of the wilderness."

Biopoem

Common Loon

Large, feathered, red-eyed, solid boned

Relative of all waterbirds

Lover of fish, diving, deep waters

Who feels unsteady on land, at home in the water, frightened of motor boats

Who needs clean water, a quiet lake, a place to nest in peace

Who fears lead sinkers, polluted waters, water skiers

Who gives a haunting cry, beauty to the world, support to its mate

Who would like to see no more acid rain, vacationers respect them, to be off the endangered list

Resident of the waterways of Canada and the United States

Loon

Advertisement:

For Sale: A Safe Place for Loons

Clear, deep, acid- and mercury-free lake stocked with fish

Ready for immediate occupancy

No fishing, boating, or water skiing allowed

Contact the Department of Wildlife at 1-800-LOON

Interview with a Male Loon

Question	Answer
What kind of loon are you?	A common loon
What do you look like?	I am large and have a low-slung body and short legs. I have black and white checkered feathers on my back, white feathers on my belly, a glossy black head, and a white necklace around my throat. My eyes are bright red, and my black bill is very long and pointed. Like other loon adults, I have a large body; mine is within the normal range of 2.7 to 6.3 kilograms. I measure almost a meter from bill tip to outstretched feet and have quite a large bill.
Does your mate look different? Explain.	My mate and I have the same plumage colorings, but I am larger.
Tell me about your bone structure.	Many of my bones are solid rather than hollow like those of other birds.
What do you eat?	I eat fish, crayfish, frogs, snails, leeches, and salamanders.
Are you a better swimmer and diver than walker? Why?	I am a much better swimmer than walker, because my body is so large, and I am so heavy that I am clumsy on land and I walk slowly. But, when I am in the water, I swim and dive with ease. My legs have powerful muscles for swimming; my heavy bones make me less buoyant and help me to dive. My large webbed feet propel me underwater, and my wings help me turn easily underwater.
Why are you sitting on the nest?	That's what loon fathers do—we take turns with loon mothers.
How many babies do you usually have each year?	Two, but lately only one egg hatches.
What kind of help will your baby need when it hatches?	Loon chicks are born already covered with down. They are able to maneuver around the nest on the first day after they are hatched, finding their own grit and pieces of vegetation. They are also able to swim within a day. After their first day or two of life, the chicks do not return to the nest. But, they spend more than half their time on their mother's and my backs to rest and conserve heat.

(Continued)

Figure 4.8 (Continued)

Diary Entry

Dear Diary,

Today my baby brother or sister died. I don't know if it was a boy or a girl because the baby never had a chance to come out of the egg. My dad was taking his turn sitting on the nest when a water skier went by. My dad got scared by the noise and the rushing water of the skier's wake, and he started to run across the water the way loons do to start their flight. When he did this, his foot hit the egg that was not yet hatched, and it cracked open. When my dad got back to the nest, he called to my mom, and together they looked at the broken egg. Then I knew I would not have a companion to grow up with. To be safe, my mom urged me up on her back, and we swam away from the ruined nest. I hope tomorrow is a better day.

Figure 4.8   Example of a Multigenre Report for Cross-Curricular Use

CHAPTER SUMMARY

As noted in the beginning of this chapter, a connection exists between reading and writing, since one must have access to written material for reading to occur, and of what use is written material unless someone reads it? Thus, in order to help students use writing to effectively learn, this chapter provides a variety of writing-to-learn strategies that can be used in all content areas.

CHAPTER 5

Speaking to Learn in Content Area Disciplines

Discussion is an exchange of knowledge.

Robert Quillen

A RATIONALE FOR SPEAKING TO LEARN

In a manner similar to that of writing to learn, speaking to learn holds an important place in the classroom. According to the Center for the Advancement of Teaching and Learning at Kansas State University, when students utilize speaking to express their learning, they

- apply the concepts they have learned.
- develop their critical thinking.
- listen carefully to one another's ideas.
- effectively communicate to and with others.
- recognize existing problems.
- acquire and use problem-solving skills.
- change their beliefs, preferences, or attitudes.
- evaluate ideas and attitudes.

- develop their interpersonal skills.

- exercise their decision-making skills.

- respect others' contributions.

- effectively participate in group actions.

- critically consider many points of view.

- retain their learning for use in future situations. (2006)

In effect, then, during the act of speaking, as in writing, students are able to not only process the ideas and concepts of their learning but also give concrete shape to those thoughts. In fact, Tama and McClain (2001) tell us that, while teachers utilize discussions to assure that students master the subjects they study, it also enables the students to analyze, explore, evaluate, and modify their attitudes on a variety of issues. And, when they are engaged in the process of discussion with others, students learn to listen to the thoughts and voices of others and to become both knowledgeable and tolerant of the opposing thoughts, viewpoints, and beliefs presented. Furthermore, Tama and McClain (2001) note that, through discussions, "students develop a tolerance for the opinions and interpretations of others, recognize that the interpretations of others will vary, learn how to cope with ambiguity, stretch the boundaries of their knowing and participate in problem solving." (pp. 300–301).

As has been established, utilizing content area discussion strategies in the classroom is an effective avenue for developing higher-level thinking abilities as well as encouraging students to broaden their perspectives as they interact with a myriad of differing points of view. However, in order for this to occur, the framework for discussions in the classroom must be carefully established and developed. Each discussion strategy selected needs to provide a goal for the learning students will achieve, so they can collaborate and discuss together with a common purpose in mind. Second, Vacca and Vacca (2008) stress the importance of keeping the discussion focused on the specific topic, question, or problem, and they suggest that, from time to time, the teacher or discussion facilitator may need to refocus the group or pose clarifying questions in order to assure that participants keep their original focus. Finally, the discussion strategies utilized must allow students to actively participate in the discussion and contribute to the quality of the conversation that results.

In addition to the selection of effective content area discussion strategies to use in the classroom, Alvermann, Dillon, and O'Brien (1987) advise that the role the teacher plays is also crucial to successful student learning. In essence, there are four possible roles a teacher can play. The first is the role of (1) the instructor, where the teacher claries any confusion or difficulties that occur as the students discuss their learning. However Alvermann et al. warn that this role can lessen the students' autonomy in maintaining their discussion effectively and resolving problems on their own. A second is the role of (2) a participant, where the teacher sits in as a partner in the discussion. In this role, Alvermann et al. suggest, the teacher's presence may discourage or even prevent some students from actively participating. A third role is that of (3) a consultant, where the teacher simply roams from group to group offering aid as requested or needed. The drawback to this role, the researchers suggest, is the possibility that the teacher will become involved with one group and neglect other groups. The final role is that of (4) a neutral observer, where the teacher remains completely silent and offers no advice, help, or suggestions to the groups as they work. This role, however, is difficult to establish with students and requires time, careful development, and implementation of the "working in group" framework and format, which must be developed by each teacher to complement the teacher's teaching styles and the students' learning styles.

SPEAKING-TO-LEARN STRATEGIES

Jigsaw Strategy

The Jigsaw is a cooperative learning technique that fosters in-depth understanding of a concept. First introduced by Aronson and Patnoe (1997), the method for using the Jigsaw is to divide a problem, article, or portion of a text into sections, one for each group member. The students who are responsible for the same section join together and form a new, temporary "expert" group whose purpose is to master the concepts in their section and to develop a strategy for teaching what they have learned to the other students in their original learning group.

The Jigsaw process improves reading comprehension and listening, promotes teamwork, and encourages each student to contribute meaningfully to a discussion, something that is difficult to achieve in a large-group discussion. Just as in a jigsaw puzzle, each piece or student's part is crucial for the completion of the final product.

Steps for the Jigsaw Strategy

1. Assign students to "home" groups of four or five students. Give each student in the home group a separated section of a text.

2. Students leave their home groups and meet in "expert" groups.

3. Expert groups read and discuss the material. They make common notes to present their understandings to the other members of their home group. Teachers may want to provide a graphic organizer for recording the information.

4. The expert groups return to their home groups to teach their portion of the materials and to learn from the other members of their home group.

Focused Jigsaw

In this variation of the Jigsaw strategy, the teacher assigns a chapter or chapters of a text. While the students will be required to read the entire assignment; the teacher plans the focus of the lesson. For example, the focus could be characters, settings, major and minor events or conflicts, problems and solutions in the narrative, causes and the effects in the story, etc.

Steps for the Focused Jigsaw

1. At the beginning of class, form groups appropriate to the activity; a group of six would be appropriate for the example in this text. Tell students they are part of a "home" group and must meet again at the end of the activity.

2. Next, distribute different colors of paper, and note what each color represents. For example, Figure 5.1 shows that students who receive a pink piece of paper are to write about school, students who receive a yellow piece of paper are to write about Gene, etc.

3. Give students a set amount of time to write individually about their topics with respect to the focus that is provided.

4. Have the students meet in "expert" groups with students who have written about the same topic. In this meeting, the expert group makes common notes to present their understandings to the other members in their home group.

5. Members of the expert groups then return to their home groups to teach their portion of the material and to learn from other members in the group.

6. One student from each home group can read the material, so students can check for accuracy.

7. Teachers can provide an extension activity as needed.

See Figure 5.1 for an example of the Focused Jigsaw.

A Separate Peace Chapter 6

1. pink = school	2. yellow = Gene	3. blue = Brinker
4. green = Quackenbush	5. orange = war	6. grey = Leper

Directions: Consider how your person, place, or event relates to this idea:

Peace Deserts Devon (Chapters 6–7)

School	Gene	Brinker
• Summer session over • Official class leaders • Mr. Ludsbury—Gene has slipped; no more gaming. • If you broke the rules, they broke you.	• Assistant crew manager for invalids • Fights with Quackenbush for Finny, self • Tells Finny he was crazy in Boston • Thinks about enlisting • Will play sports for Finny	• Accuses Gene of maiming Finny • Takes Gene to the Butt Room, mock trial • Writes a poem about war • Will enlist
Quackenbush	War	Leper
• Takes his job as crew manager seriously • Confronts Gene and fights with him in Naguamsett River	• References to the year 1942 • Snow comes and paralyzes the railroad; boys must shovel so troops can get through • Soldiers are not much older than the boys	• Does not volunteer to shovel • Goes skiing to see the beaver dam • Always a fight for him

Figure 5.1   Example of a Focused Jigsaw for English

Focus Cards

Reading is an activity with a purpose. A person may read in order to gain information, verify existing knowledge, or critique a writer's ideas or writing style. A person may also read for enjoyment or to enhance knowledge of the language. The various purposes for reading guide the reader's selection of texts.

When students have a purpose for reading a selection, they find that the purpose not only directs their reading toward a goal but helps to focus their attention. Purposes may come from teacher-directed questions, questions from class discussions, brainstorming, or even particular concepts in the lesson, like the examples that follow.

A focus is the spotlight the teacher selects for students to place their attention. By using Focus Cards, a teacher can pinpoint particular concepts in a lesson. Focus Cards can be developed for a number of reasons and/or purposes, such as the following:

- Concentrating on a core concept (e.g., by focusing on a specific part of a lesson)
- Reviewing a unit
- Meeting student needs (i.e., by focusing on learning styles)
- Providing a source of directions
- Providing scaffolding

Steps for the Focus Cards Strategy

1. Before class, prepare focus cards as appropriate.

2. As class begins, distribute Focus Card(s) to students as they enter the classroom, from a designated area in the classroom, or from their assigned seats.

3. Next, students work individually or in small discussion groups to complete the Focus Cards activity.

4. When students have completed their tasks, they may complete an extension activity as well.

5. At the end of the activity, have students turn in the completed individual and group answers focus card(s).

See Figure 5.2 for an example of a Focus Cards strategy for English, Figure 5.3 for an example for mathematics, and Figure 5.4 for an example for social studies.

---

1. **Prior to Class:** The teacher prepares Focus Cards that identify specific conflicts that occur in a novel.

2. **Beginning of Class:** The teacher distributes the cards and asks the students to complete the cards, using the model as an example.

3. **Group Activity:** When the students are finished, they should share their answers with the whole class or with small groups of students.

4. **Extension Activity:** Teachers can ask students to write an essay based on the topics or use the questions as part of a review for another discussion or for a test.

Example: *The Power of One* (Chapter 10)

Conflicts: prejudice, freedom, communication change, demons, propaganda, coincidence, violence

Complete the Focus Card as follows:

1. Write the conflict (from the list above) in the middle of the card.
2. In the upper left corner, write the connection between this conflict and Chapter 10 of *The Power of One.*
3. In the lower left corner, write the names of the characters involved in this conflict.
4. In the upper right corner, write a quotation from Chapter 10 that reflects this conflict.
5. In the lower right corner, draw a symbol for this conflict.

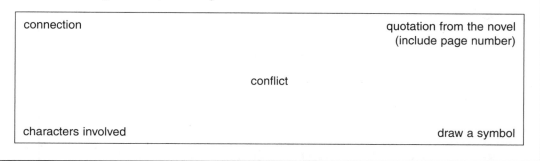

connection	quotation from the novel (include page number)
	conflict	
characters involved	draw a symbol

Figure 5.2 Example of Focus Cards for Literature: Conflicts

1. **Prior to Class:** The teacher prepares focus cards with narrative measurement problems of various degrees of difficulty and steps, keeping in mind student ability. Focus cards are numbered by the teacher to predetermine groups. Groups can be formed in a number of ways; for example they may be homogenous or heterogeneous according to ability, they may group students with similar or different learning styles, or they may be organized according to problem type.

2. **Beginning of Class:** The teacher distributes focus cards to the students. Tools to complete measurement problems are provided, for example, rulers, tape measures, cups, tablespoons, teaspoons, etc. Students are directed to form groups according to the number on their Focus Card.

3. **Group Activity:**
   a. If all students in the small group have the same problem, the group works together to solve it. Either by the teacher or by the group, one student is assigned to read the problem, one student writes the problem in numbers, one student agrees to report the results to the whole class, and one or more students complete the problem activity; for example, they measure the perimeter of your desk, determine the area of a book, etc.
   b. If each student has a different measurement problem to solve, they work independently in the group with the given tools, solve the problem, and then share their solutions with each other. Group members check each problem's solution to determine whether it is correct and whether the tools used to solve the problem were appropriate.
   c. Each group provides its solutions to the teacher for feedback at the end of the activity.

4. **Extension Activity:** Students create their own measurement problem for others to solve or they create and solve a measurement problem which can be completed at home.

Figure 5.3 Example of Focus Cards for Mathematics: Problems With Measurement

These activities, which are based on Bloom's Taxonomy, vary in complexity and time allotment.

1. **Prior to Class:** Use different colors of paper to prepare several copies of five different Focus Cards:
   a. (Knowledge) Recall the source where the history of Judaism began.
   b. (Comprehension) Discuss the reasons that Israel is central to Judaism.
   c. (Analysis) Explain how Jews regard the idea of living outside of Israel.
   d. (Evaluation) Justify the reasons for selecting Israel as a Jewish state.
   e. (Synthesis) How would the relationships between Christians and Jews change if a different country had been chosen to be a Jewish state?

2. **Beginning of Class:** Distribute colored paper Focus Cards as the students enter the classroom; each student should get one of the five cards. Ask students to work by themselves to complete the assignments on their individual cards. Provide help as needed, and give each student a completion grade when the student indicates his or her work is complete.

3. **Group Activity:** Students work with other students who have the same assignment and compare their answers. Then students from each group volunteer to share their answers with the class.

Figure 5.4   Example of Focus Cards for Social Studies: Israel as Jewish State

First Thoughts Strategy

Many learners who should do well in a subject actually underperform, because the new material seems irrelevant. When prior learning is activated, the brain is more likely to make connections to the information, thus increasing comprehension and meaning (Jensen, 2000). The more background students have, the more connections they will make.

In order to prepare students for a lesson and to increase individual accountability, have students answer a question, solve a problem, define a term, or jot down their ideas before a class activity or discussion.

Steps for the First Thoughts Strategy

1. Give students three to five minutes to respond to a question, solve a problem, identify a term, or jot down their ideas.

2. Encourage the students to respond to the prompt by noting their first thoughts and by making associations and connections to the prompt.

3. After students write, have them share their responses with a partner, in a small group, or with the whole class.

See Figure 5.5 for examples of prompts for the First Thoughts strategy.

Prompt Type	Example Prompt
Question	Why do we have daylight savings time?
Problem to be solved	How can we improve security in the building?
Term	*irritating* List three things that you consider irritating. Why do they irritate you?
Idea	Explain why the main character is prejudiced.

Figure 5.5   Examples of Prompts for First Thoughts Strategy

Content-Focused Drama

Content-Focused Drama, described by Cooter and Chilcoat (1991), is an exciting combination of writing, speaking, and listening that students craft into a melodrama about a topic they have studied. Working in small groups, students use the facts they have learned about a topic to create a story line, develop appropriate characters, and even design the scenery necessary to perform a play about some aspect of that topic.

Steps for Content-Focused Drama

Cooter and Chilcoat (1991) suggest that students proceed through the following stages as they develop their Content-Focused Drama:

1. First, students organize the facts they have gleaned from their research of the topic.

2. Next, they choose the aspect of the topic they will develop for their drama and create appropriate characters.

3. Then they compose the script to tell the story.

4. Finally, students revise and edit the script into its final form.

As students work to creatively write the script, Cooter and Chilcoat (1991) strongly urge that they adhere to and utilize the elements of a true melodrama, such as stereotypical characters who are larger-than-life heroes, supervillains, nasty cads, and steamy loves as well as overly dramatic acting and lots of bustling action.

Literature Circles

A Literature Circle is a student-centered reading activity for a group of four to six students who have chosen to read the same piece of literature. Each member of a circle agrees to take a specific responsibility during discussion. Literature circles meet on a regular basis, and the discussion roles change at each meeting (Daniels, 2002). Daniels believes in introducing literature circles by using predefined roles that students take turns fulfilling. Although the terminology used to name the roles may vary, the descriptions remain similar. Students should write their responses on teacher-prepared handouts or in a notebook or a journal.

Literature Circle Roles

Discussion Director: develops questions for the group to answer

Literary Luminary: selects interesting passages and quotations to discuss

Vocabulary Enricher: chooses words that are difficult or used in an unfamiliar way

Text Connector: finds connections between the reading material and something outside the text, such as a personal experience, a related issue in the news, or a topic from another text

Illustrator: draws one or more pictures that relate to the reading

Steps for Literature Circles

1. Students form groups based on their interests.

2. Groups decide how many pages to read, choose a role for each group member, and set a date for the first meeting and discussion.

3. Observe the groups, and act as a facilitator if needed.

4. Teachers can collect the students' responses, and respond to them as needed.

The Literary Tea Party

As human beings, we rely and depend on one another. In fact, according to Jensen (2000) our very survival depends upon our relationships with others. Therefore, it is crucial to make sure that every learner develops the necessary set of social skills to interact properly in the world. Humans cannot grow up isolated and be expected to succeed in society. Students learn more when they are actively involved in learning. Activities like plays, skits, debates, games, and the tea party activate learning.

The Literary Tea Party strategy, which has its origins in Britain in the early 1800s, can be a wonderful experience for students, especially when it is combined with lessons on history, literature, and manners. Teachers can plan a simple Literary Tea Party like the one below or incorporate the social aspect of having tea into a research assignment.

Steps for the Literary Tea Party Strategy

1. Choose a novel that focuses on a particular time period or cultural setting. Some suggestions: *The Great Gatsby, To Kill a Mockingbird, The Count of Monte*

Cristo, A Doll's House, The Glass Menagerie, A Farewell to Arms, and any novel from Victorian literature.

2. Invite students to a tea to share their ideas about a character in the novel. Include the criteria for the assignment in the invitation. Alternatively, students can write invitations to each other.

3. Criteria for the assignment can include the following:

   a. Students are randomly assigned a character from the novel, or they can choose their own character.

   b. Students assume the identity of the character. They must be familiar with the character's status and role in the novel and his or her relationships with other characters. Since students will share their discussion with another character or characters, teachers might provide some time for students to practice behaving like their characters.

   c. On the day the assignment is due, students sit in small groups, drink tea, and share their roles by behaving like their characters. Students might also bring food to share at the tea party that is representative of the culture or time period represented in the novel.

   d. Students can also be required to dress like their character or bring an object that represents their character.

A Variation: The Victorian Tea Party and Research

Steps for the Victorian Tea Party Strategy and Research

1. Each student selects and researches a specific British author. Students could research some of the following ideas: background information, struggles in life, significant accomplishments, relevance to the time period, relationships with other authors, etc.

2. To prepare for the tea, the student, playing the role of the author, reports on the author by responding as the author would respond to questions posed by the teacher and other members of the class.

3. Before the day of the tea, the teacher can select a master of ceremonies from the list of authors.

4. On the day of the tea, the master of ceremonies introduces each "author" to Queen Victoria, who is usually impersonated by the teacher.

5. During the tea, the students play the parts of their authors and share their author research with other members of the class. The students may bring information on an index card and must bring a three-dimensional prop. .

6. To make the tea more realistic, the students may sign up to bring authentic British tea and food, including cucumber sandwiches, biscuits, scones or shortbread with lemon curd, ice cream, and pudding.

7. And, of course, students must follow proper etiquette during the tea.

Circle of Knowledge

The Circle of Knowledge strategy is highly motivating and is ideal for reinforcing skills in any subject area. It provides a framework for review in which everyone learns more or confirms what he or she has already mastered. The strategy involves posing a question to the whole class, then moving into cooperative learning groups for additional examination of the issues, and then moving back to the whole class for further discussion. This teaching strategy engages all students in an interactive model (Silver, Strong, & Perini, 2007).

Steps to the Circle of Knowledge Strategy

1. Position several small teams of four or five students in circles around a room. Have each team appoint one student as the recorder.

2. Pose a single question or problem that has many possible answers.

3. Have each team respond to the question simultaneously but quietly:

    a. A member in each team is selected as the first to begin, and answers to the problem posed are then provided by one member at a time, taking turns and moving clockwise or counterclockwise around the circle.

    b. No member may skip his turn, and no one may provide an answer until the person directly before him has delivered his; therefore, the answers stop while a member is thinking of a possible reply.

    c. No teammate may give an answer to another, but teammates may pantomime hints to assist the person whose turn it is.

    d. The recorder writes each person's answer on a sheet of paper. Only the recorder may write.

    e. At the end of a predetermined time, stop the process, and record the number of responses that each team has generated.

4. Using newsprint, a whiteboard, a chalkboard, or an overhead, draw a table that all students can see that includes columns to identify and represent each team.

5. In turn, have a representative from each team offer one of the answers suggested by that representative's team. When an answer is provided, write it in that team's column.

6. As you write each answer, all recorders look over their list of answers, and if that answer appears on their lists, the recorder crosses it off, thus gradually decreasing the length of the list so that only the answers that have not yet been reported remain. This process continues until no team has any remaining answers on its list.

7. Award points for each answer at your discretion, and allow rival teams to challenge each other's answers.

8. If an answer is challenged, you as teacher must decide if the answer is correct. If the answer is right and the challenger incorrect, the challenger's team loses the number of points given for one correct answer. If the answer is incorrect and the challenger was right, the team that provided the answer loses the point(s), and the challenger's team gains it (them).

9. Discuss the results with the class, or ask the class to reflect on what they have learned or reaffirmed as a result of the activity.

Questions in Styles

Another effective discussion strategy is Questions in Styles. Silver, Strong, & Perini (2001) note that in order to help students gather and make sense of various types of information, they need to be able to employ four elements of critical thinking: recalling, reasoning, reorganizing and applying, and, finally, relating personally. In the strategy Questions in Styles, Silver et al. (2001) have developed a simple and powerful critical thinking tool that enables students to first gain practice and then independence in using four types of questions: (1) mastery questions, which require students to recall and gather information about a topic; (2) understanding questions, which require students to apply their reasoning skills to draw logical conclusions and make inferences for their study of a topic; (3) interpersonal questions, which ask students to personally express their feelings about the value of the topic of study; and (4) self-expressive questions, which require students to reorganize, speculate about, and apply the information they are learning to solve problems.

To understand the parameters of each of these four questioning types, Silver et al. (2001) and Tama and McClain (2001) provide the following question menu:

1. Questions that reflect the mastery aspect include the following:
   a. Who?
   b. What?
   c. Where?
   d. When?
   e. How?
   f. What did you observe?
   g. Describe the characteristics of what you observed.
   h. Develop a timeline of or a list of steps for what you learned.

2. Questions that reflect the understanding aspect include the following:
   a. What was the main idea of the reading?
   b. What were the important points presented in the reading?
   c. What are the similarities and differences?
   d. What are the causes and effects?

    e. Can you explain what you have read about?

    f. Can you provide specific evidence from the real world to substantiate what you have read about?

    g. Are there any hidden assumptions that you as the reader can make as a result of your reading?

    h. Have you made a discovery from what you have read, and can you provide evidence about this discovery from the real world?

3. Questions that reflect the interpersonal aspect include:

    a. How would you feel if _____?

    b. How do you think _____ felt?

    c. Why is _____ important to you?

    d. Why is _____ of value to you?

    e. How would you advise or console _____?

    f. How would you help each side come to consensus?

    g. Given a choice on this topic, what would you do?

    h. Are there alternative solutions to the problem? If so, what are the consequences of using each of them?

    i. Do you think your solution is the best one? If so, explain.

4. Questions that reflect the self-expressive aspect include:

    a. How is _____ like _____?

    b. What would happen if _____?

    c. Suppose _____; what would it look like? What might be the consequences?

    d. What do you think will happen next?

    e. Given the data you gleaned from the reading, develop a plan of action to address the issue in the reading.

Adroitly using all of these four types of questions enables students to "explore the multiple layers of meaning in the content they are studying" (Silver et al., 2001, p. 126).

Steps for the Questions in Styles Strategy

1. Provide students with an assignment to read and a set of question stems that match the four types of critical thinking and learning styles discussed above.

2. Have students study each question stem and identify its type.

3. Next, students reread the text assignment and gather the information needed to successfully answer the questions and develop appropriate answers.

4. Then, in small groups, students share and discuss their responses.

5. Finally, students reflect on the various styles of questions they encountered, indicate which one they preferred, and explain why.

Tama and McClain (2001) offer an interesting variation on the Questions in Styles strategy in another strategy they call Questions in 4 Learning Styles. While the questions posed to students are basically the same as those shown above, the authors suggest that, instead of asking students to answer and discuss all four types, students peruse the question types and choose the type that they feel most matches their learning style. This is obviously a valid variation and would, in our opinion, be an excellent way to introduce this strategy, since it allows students to successfully answer a question at their comfort level. Then, once students become adroit at their chosen question style, they may be encouraged to attempt the other three types of questions.

See Figure 5.6 for a set of Questions in Styles for science and Figure 5.9 on page 113 for a reproducible master for Questions in Styles.

Mastery Questions	Interpersonal Questions
• What is global warming? • Describe global warming. • Where it is occurring? • How extensive is it? • Have you observed it? • Develop a timeline of its effects.	• How would you feel if you were a polar bear and your iceberg was melting? • Why is the concept of global warming important or of value to you? • What advice can you give on global warming? • How would you help opposing sides come to consensus on global warming? • What are alternative solutions to global warming, and what are their consequences? • Is your solution is the best one? If so, explain.
Understanding Questions	Self-Expressive Questions
• What was the main idea of the reading? • What important points about global warming does the reading present? • What are the causes and effects of global warming? • What specific evidence of global warming was presented? • Can you make assumptions about global warming from what you have read? • Have you made any new discoveries about global warming, and can you prove them?	• How is global warming like an ice cube? • Suppose global warming was accelerated? What would it look like? What might be the consequences? • What do you think will happen next if we ignore the problem of global warming? • Develop a plan of action to stop or slow down global warming.

Figure 5.6 Example of Questions in Styles for Science

Discussion Web

The Discussion Web (Alvermann, 1991) is a strategy that encourages students to examine an issue from alternative viewpoints, thereby fostering reflection and critical thinking while promoting active discussion. To utilize this strategy, students read an assignment, listen to a lecture, or view a video or CD and are then asked to respond to a controversial question about the content of the presentation or reading. They are asked to consider both the reasons for and the reasons against the response they choose, and to record their response and reasons on a graphic organizer. Then, first in pairs and then in fours, the students discuss the reasons they have identified for and against their conclusions and to come to a consensus conclusion, which they also record on a graphic organizer. The Discussion Web strategy is especially effective, because it requires that students first reflect on the question and clarify their own position on it before they meet with others to share their lists of pro and con responses to the question. Once the lists have been shared with others, the students must reach a consensus as to which viewpoint they will all support and provide a single reason for their decision. Once all groups have reached consensus, they report their findings to the entire class. As always, the teacher should model this strategy for students.

Steps for a Discussion Web

1. Place students in pairs, and provide each with a copy of the Discussion Web graphic organizer.

2. After students have read the assignment, pose a controversial question for them to consider.

3. Ask students to consider both sides of the controversial issue and record the reasons for and against it in the appropriate sections of the graphic organizer. Remind students that they should try to provide an equal number of reasons for and against their position.

4. When students have completed their organizers individually, ask them to compare their responses with those of their partner, discuss the evidence they have gathered for each side of the argument and reach a consensus on which position they prefer.

5. Next, ask each pair to join another pair of students to compare and discuss the evidence they have gathered for both sides of the question. This group of four will now reach a consensus on the controversial question and provide a single, best reason to support their decision. Remind them that if they do not agree on one conclusion, they must choose a conclusion most of them agree on.

6. Finally, ask one student from each group of four to present the group's consensus decision and one reason for choosing that decision. (Note: To

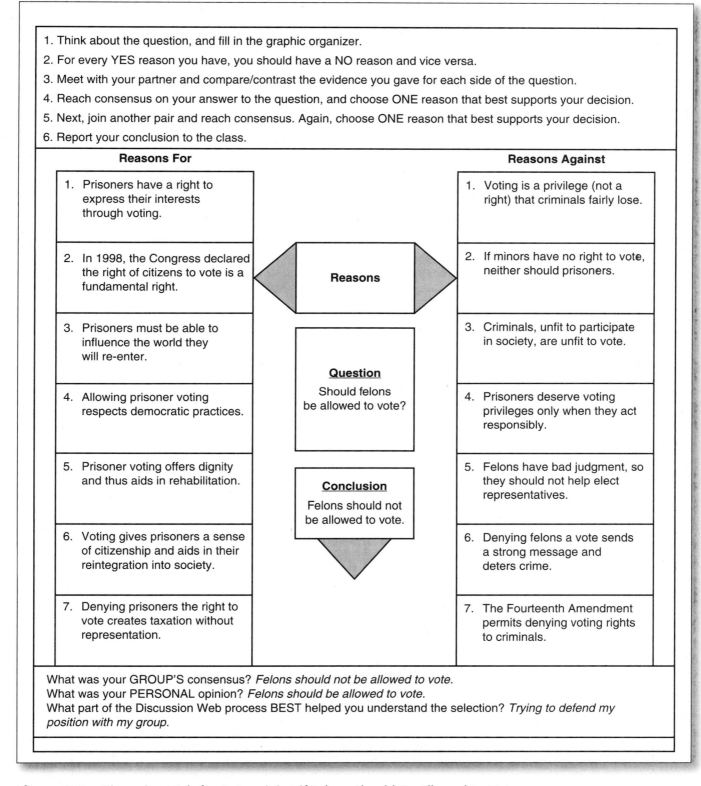

1. Think about the question, and fill in the graphic organizer.
2. For every YES reason you have, you should have a NO reason and vice versa.
3. Meet with your partner and compare/contrast the evidence you gave for each side of the question.
4. Reach consensus on your answer to the question, and choose ONE reason that best supports your decision.
5. Next, join another pair and reach consensus. Again, choose ONE reason that best supports your decision.
6. Report your conclusion to the class.

Reasons For

1. Prisoners have a right to express their interests through voting.

2. In 1998, the Congress declared the right of citizens to vote is a fundamental right.

3. Prisoners must be able to influence the world they will re-enter.

4. Allowing prisoner voting respects democratic practices.

5. Prisoner voting offers dignity and thus aids in rehabilitation.

6. Voting gives prisoners a sense of citizenship and aids in their reintegration into society.

7. Denying prisoners the right to vote creates taxation without representation.

Reasons

Question
Should felons be allowed to vote?

Conclusion
Felons should not be allowed to vote.

Reasons Against

1. Voting is a privilege (not a right) that criminals fairly lose.

2. If minors have no right to vote, neither should prisoners.

3. Criminals, unfit to participate in society, are unfit to vote.

4. Prisoners deserve voting privileges only when they act responsibly.

5. Felons have bad judgment, so they should not help elect representatives.

6. Denying felons a vote sends a strong message and deters crime.

7. The Fourteenth Amendment permits denying voting rights to criminals.

What was your GROUP'S consensus? *Felons should not be allowed to vote.*
What was your PERSONAL opinion? *Felons should be allowed to vote.*
What part of the Discussion Web process BEST helped you understand the selection? *Trying to defend my position with my group.*

Figure 5.7 Discussion Web for Determining if Felons Should Be Allowed to Vote

SOURCE: Based on Alvermann (1991).

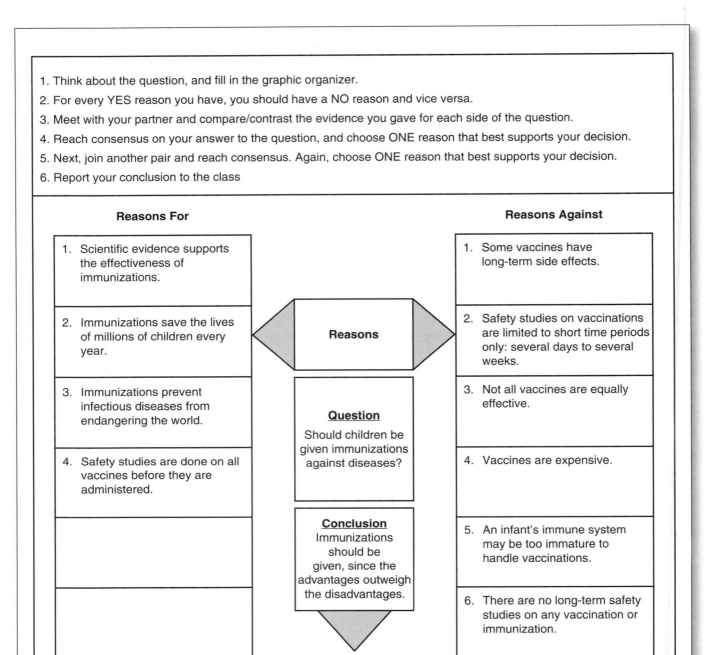

1. Think about the question, and fill in the graphic organizer.

2. For every YES reason you have, you should have a NO reason and vice versa.

3. Meet with your partner and compare/contrast the evidence you gave for each side of the question.

4. Reach consensus on your answer to the question, and choose ONE reason that best supports your decision.

5. Next, join another pair and reach consensus. Again, choose ONE reason that best supports your decision.

6. Report your conclusion to the class

Reasons For

1. Scientific evidence supports the effectiveness of immunizations.

2. Immunizations save the lives of millions of children every year.

3. Immunizations prevent infectious diseases from endangering the world.

4. Safety studies are done on all vaccines before they are administered.

Reasons

Question
Should children be given immunizations against diseases?

Conclusion
Immunizations should be given, since the advantages outweigh the disadvantages.

Reasons Against

1. Some vaccines have long-term side effects.

2. Safety studies on vaccinations are limited to short time periods only: several days to several weeks.

3. Not all vaccines are equally effective.

4. Vaccines are expensive.

5. An infant's immune system may be too immature to handle vaccinations.

6. There are no long-term safety studies on any vaccination or immunization.

What was your GROUP'S consensus? *Immunizations should be given.*
What was your PERSONAL opinion? *Immunizations should be given.*
What part of the Discussion Web process BEST helped you understand the selection? *Trying to defend my position with my group.*

Figure 5.8   Discussion Web for Determining if Immunizations Should Be Given to Children

SOURCE: Based on Alvermann (1991).

facilitate the presentations, ask students to prioritize all the reasons for their decision so if their first reason has been reported by another group, they can provide their "next best" reason. This gives students practice in prioritizing and eliminates the possibility that groups who report later in the class period will have no viable reasons left to share.)

7. To help students reflect on how the Discussion Web strategy facilitated their learning, ask students to respond to the following questions:

    a. What conclusion did you personally come to?

    b. What is the best reason to support this conclusion?

    c. Did focusing on a question before you read help you understand the reading better?

    d. Did searching for evidence as you read help you understand the reading better?

    e. What was the most difficult step of the process? Why?

    f. Which step do you think best helped you understand? Explain.

    g. Did you change your mind about the question during any step of the process? Explain.

This strategy can be used in any content area. For example, in social studies, students can consider whether war criminals from World War II should still be tried now, more than 60 years after their crimes were committed; in science, they can argue for or against restrictions on drilling for oil or cutting down trees in order to save endangered species; in English, they can consider whether Ethan Frome deserved the life he got after his wife's accident; and, finally, in health classes they can consider whether mandatory drug testing should be required of all school athletes. Figure 5.7 presents an example of a Discussion Web for social studies, while Figure 5.8 presents an example for science. Figure 5.10 at the end of the chapter is a reproducible master to use with this strategy.

Save the Last Word for Me

A strategy that is specifically designed to encourage both critical and reflective thinking and learning is Save the Last Word for Me (Burke and Harste as discussed in Buehl, 2001). According to Buehl, this strategy is best utilized when the reading assigned might elicit differing interpretations or opinions from students. Furthermore, the strategy is most successful when conducted in a small-group setting rather than in a whole-class setting, because some students are reluctant to share their differing or opposing ideas and opinions in front of a large group. In addition, the fact that this strategy asks students to prepare their thoughts and reflections ahead of time by writing them down on index cards provides all students some rehearsal time to prepare before they are asked to present, which will make speaking more comfortable even for the most reluctant ones.

Steps for Save the Last Word for Me

1. After reading either an expository or narrative assignment, have students identify at least five statements that they deem interesting; that are contradictory to their thoughts, beliefs, or established knowledge; that surprised or intrigued them; or that in some way revealed new knowledge to them. Have them record each of the five statements and its location in the reading assignment on the front side of an index card.

2. On the back side of the index card, ask students to record their thoughts and reflections about each of the five statements and to indicate why they chose the statements.

3. Once the index cards have been completed, place students into small groups, assign each student a number, and instruct students to share their statements according to the following format:

   a. Student #1 chooses one of her statements and provides its location, so all members of the group may read it.

   b. When all group members have read the statement, each one, in turn, comments on it by agreeing with, refuting, supporting, clarifying, commenting, or questioning the statement.

   c. After listening to all the group members' thoughts and reflections, student #1 shares her thoughts and reflections, thereby "saving the last word for me." As Buehl states, "The attitude during this phase is: Here is a statement that interested me. You tell me what you think, and then I will tell you what I think" (p. 122).

   d. This process of sharing thoughts and reflections then continues with the rest of the students until all of the statements have been presented.

Below is an example of Save the Last Word for Me for narrative writing.

The Statement: "As the door opened I knew I had to go in, but, I also knew everyone would stare at me. It was just human nature!"

The Last Word: The statement, "It was just human nature" really made me wonder why, even though we know how people will feel if we react to something, we just do it anyway. In the story, the main character was going to feel embarrassed, but people stared anyway and then just blamed it on human nature. Sometimes acting like a human means acting in a cruel way. I wish people would think before they act like humans!

And here is an example for expository writing.

The Statement: "On Christmas Eve, three boys who were members of a Hull House club were killed as they worked in a factory because no guard had been hired to watch them, and when the incident was reported to the factory owners, they showed no remorse."

The Last Word: I was aware of the terrible conditions that faced child laborers, but I did not know how cruel and thoughtless the owners were. How could they sleep at night knowing that children were in constant danger? And, why did they fail to hire a guard? Did it cost too much? Was the cost of a guard more important than the lives of three children? Finally, how did they break the news to the children's parents, especially on Christmas Eve?

Intra-Act

Another strategy that fosters students' ability for critical and reflective thinking and learning is Intra-Act (Hoffman, 1979). In this strategy, students are called to engage their affective domain by personally reflecting and reacting to value statements that are based on the content they have read. As Tama and McClain (2001) note, this strategy allows students not only to discuss what has been read but to strengthen and extend their thinking by taking a chance and voicing their personal reactions and clarifying their values regarding the reading. This, they stress, encourages all students to be tolerant to the reactions and values of others.

Vacca and Vacca (2008) warn that, before the Intra-Act strategy is initiated, the teacher must be sure to follow effective prereading procedures by introducing the text to be read, fostering the students' prior knowledge, and encouraging students to make predictions about the content to be read, so students have a frame of reference for what they are to read and react to.

Steps for Intra-Act

1. Once the students have been introduced to and have read the text to be discussed, group them into teams of four to six, and ask them to select a team leader.

2. The team leader then provides a summary of the selection and elicits additional information, clarification, and questions from the other members of the group. Ideally, this discussion should last no more than ten minutes.

3. Next the team leader encourages students to share their personal reactions and value judgments. Again, this should last no more than ten minutes.

4. Once all members of the group have shared their personal reactions and value judgments, they are ready to participate in the valuing portion of the strategy. In this phase, give students a set of four value statements you have developed that provide opinions and insights about the text's content. Students then denote their personal value judgments by agreeing or disagreeing with each statement as well as predicting how the other members of the group will respond. Students can record their statements and predictions on a graphic organizer, such as the one in Figure 5.11.

5. Next, each student reveals how he or she responded to each statement, and other members of the group check their predictions of each other's responses.

6. Finally, students discuss the results, reflect on what led to the predictions they made, and consider whether those perceptions were, indeed, correct.

Overall, as noted earlier, this strategy fosters not only a clarification of what was studied but encourages all students to be tolerant to the reactions and values of others. As with Save the Last Word for Me, Intra-Act can be used with both narrative and expository texts. Below is an example of a value statement for Intra-Act for narrative writing.

The Statement: In *To Kill A Mockingbird,* Tom Robinson should not have run away. He should have waited until his trial.

And here is an example for expository writing.

The Statement: Even if the farmers of Brazil need land to farm on, they should not slash and burn the jungle, since the wildfires destroy exotic plants and animals.

See Figure 5.11 on page 115 for a reproducible master for the Intra-Act strategy.

CHAPTER SUMMARY

As noted in the beginning of this chapter, speaking to learn holds an important place in the classroom, for when students use speaking, they are able to process the ideas and concepts they learn and give shape to them. Thus, in order to help students use speaking to effectively learn, this chapter provides a variety of speaking-to-learn strategies that can be used in all content areas.

QUESTIONS IN STYLES

Questions in Styles for _____

Mastery Questions	Interpersonal Questions
Understanding Questions	**Self-Expressive Questions**

Figure 5.9   Reproducible Master for Questions in Styles

DISCUSSION WEB STRATEGY

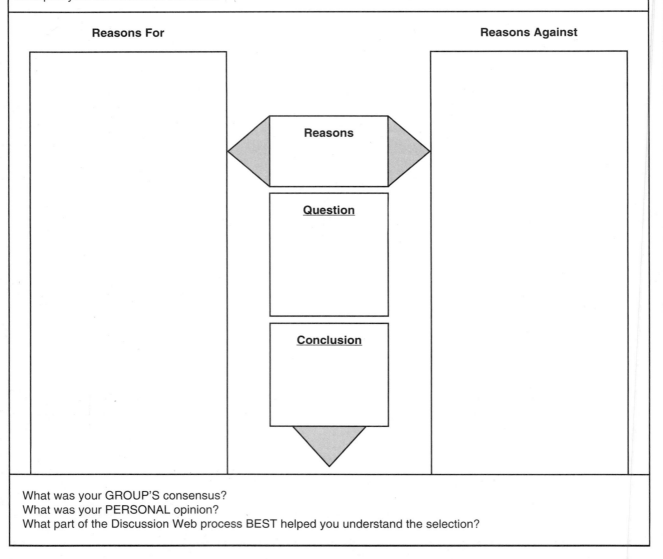

1. Think about the question, and fill in the graphic organizer.
2. For every YES reason you have, you should have a NO reason and vice versa.
3. Meet with your partner and compare/contrast the evidence you gave for each side of the question.
4. Reach consensus on whether you agree or disagree with the position statement, and choose ONE reason that best supports your decision.
5. Next, join another pair and reach consensus. Again, choose ONE reason that best supports your decision.
6. Report your conclusion to the class.

Reasons For   Reasons Against

Reasons

Question

Conclusion

What was your GROUP'S consensus?
What was your PERSONAL opinion?
What part of the Discussion Web process BEST helped you understand the selection?

Figure 5.10   Reproducible Master for the Discussion Web Strategy

SOURCE: Based on Alvermann (1991). From *Reading and Writing Across Content Areas* (2nd ed., p. 181), by R. L. Sejnost and S. Thiese, 2007, Thousand Oaks, CA: Corwin. Copyright © 2007 by Corwin. Reprinted with permission.

INTRA-ACT

Name _____ Date _____ Topic _____

Teacher Developed Value Statements	Student 1 Reaction		Student 2 Reaction		Student 3 Reaction		Student 4 Reaction	
1.	A	D	A	D	A	D	A	D
2.	A	D	A	D	A	D	A	D
3.	A	D	A	D	A	D	A	D
4.	A	D	A	D	A	D	A	D

Figure 5.11   Reproducible Master for Intra-Act

CHAPTER 6

Fostering Real World Literacy

*We must prepare young people for living in a world
of powerful images, words, and sounds.*

UNESCO, 1982

THE LITERACIES OF THE REAL WORLD

No one who works with the students of today can deny the fact that these students are faced with the need to learn new literacies that students of yesteryear never saw. Leu, Kinzer, Coiro, and Cammack (2004) remind us that the traditional conceptions we once held of print are quickly being replaced by much broader conceptions of literacy that are influenced by information and communication technologies. In effect, these emerging technologies, the media, and the Internet are changing what it means to be literate. The digital age is transforming the quantity, range, and speed of information and communication in our lives, and new media are affecting how we understand the world. And, Leu and Leu (2000) and Kist (2005) stress, these new literacies are what is necessary for students to effectively meet the conceptual and technological demands that will be made on them in the 21st century. Thus, the need to incorporate a wider range of learning philosophies is evident in classrooms because, as Leu, Leu, and Coiro (2006) tell us, new literacies provide students with opportunities "to identify important questions, navigate complex information networks to locate important information, critically evaluate that information, synthesize it to address those questions and then communicate the answers to others" (p. 1).

The goal of the teacher, then, is to expand the choices available to students to help them become better readers and learners. And, Vacca and Vacca (2008) stress, to do this, teachers must help students "learn how to learn new technologies" (p. 420) and provide instructional support for them, so they can develop and use strategies, especially those that enable them to read critically and evaluate information. Overall, then, as teachers we must help students understand and deal with the many faces of these new literacies, such as information literacy, which places an emphasis on the ability to identify, know, evaluate, and use information; and media and visual literacy, which are often related to popular culture and are associated with the ability to interpret and analyze images. If we do this, we will equip them to be learners in the real world of today's digital age. And, no one can deny that one of the foundations of the digital age is the Internet.

THE INTERNET

The Internet has had an amazing influence on the students, and this influence is growing. Today's adolescents live in a world surrounded by communication technologies: The Internet, iPods, and cell phones and are essential components of their lives. A study completed in 2004 by the Henry J. Kaiser Family Foundation revealed that 96% of all children between 8 and 18 have used the Internet at least once (Ruddell, 2006). And, according to the Pew Research Center, the number of teenagers using the Internet has grown 24% in the past four years, and 87% of those between the ages of 12 and 17 go online regularly (Lenhart, Hitlin, & Madden, 2004). The use of the Internet has also expanded in the number of teens who play games; shop; use Facebook, Twitter, and MySpace; and access information online.

This use of the Internet, according to Vacca and Vacca (2008), can serve students in a variety of ways by providing motivation to read, unlimited access to information, and far-reaching opportunities for communication. Leu (2002) and Reinking (2003), as found in Vacca and Vacca (2008), note that when students use the Internet, their interest in and motivation for reading is increased. Second, Vacca and Vacca (2008) point out that the vast world of the Web provides students with access to a plethora of texts on every possible subject, because they have access to a hypermedia system, in essence a "universe of servers (computers)" (p. 431). Finally, students with access to the Internet have access to a system of communication that allows them to communicate with the entire world quickly and efficiently. Overall, one cannot deny that access to the Internet presents students with unlimited learning opportunities. However, Vacca and Vacca (2008) stress that if students are to use the Internet to it fullest potential, we must be sure that they become experts at browsing and surfing the Net so that they "develop the strategic knowledge, skills, and insights that will take them beyond trivial and superficial learning" (p. 430). In addition, they must be able to adequately evaluate the Web sites they browse. The following section will provide information on how to accomplish that.

Evaluating Web Sources

Today, our students typically begin their information experiences on the Internet, where materials can be published by anyone on any subject. If students have been taught only to read and understand this information, they could be in serious trouble. Memorizing facts and information is not the most important skill in today's world. Facts change, and information is readily available; what is needed is an understanding of how to get and make sense of the mass of data. Accessing information in an increasingly digital world involves an array of skills of which decoding text is only a small part. Basic skills for today's students include locating, organizing, and evaluating relevant information. Establishing the validity, authorship, timeliness, and integrity of what one finds is a critical part of the process. Four criteria for evaluating Web sites are:

Accuracy

- Who wrote the information?
- What is the purpose of the publication?
- What are the qualifications of the person writing?

Authority

- Look at the URL to find an author or editor or the publishers.
- Make sure the author's credentials are credible.

Currency

- Check the publication date and updates.

Content

- Is the information organized and readable?
- Is the information complete and relevant to the topic?
- Is the information linked to other sources?
- Is the information objective?

Guidelines for Creating Effective Internet Activities

Informational literacy includes more than just choosing effective Web sources, and it is best taught in close integration with content or subject areas. In addition, teachers must be aware of the standards developed for teaching about technology by the International Society for Technology in 2008. These are as follows:

1. Facilitate experiences that promote student learning and creativity.
2. Design, develop, and assess authentic digital learning experiences to maximize learning.

3. Illustrate different ways to use digital-age technology.

4. Promote and exhibit ethical behavior using digital resources.

5. Engage in professional growth and leadership practices.

In addition, while the draw of the Internet is great, Coulter, Feldman, and Konold (2000) remind us that "the Internet is no silver bullet for improving education" (p. 43) and encourage teachers to consider the advantage of Internet activities in relation to other means of teaching the information. To facilitate this, they provide a set of items to consider before choosing to utilize the Internet as an instructional tool. These are as follows:

- Clearly identify the curriculum-related purpose of the planned activities. In other words, the assigned activity must accomplish an objective or standard in the school curriculum.

- Consider if the use of the Internet will enhance the activity.

- Make sure students use the Internet sources they have located in some way. It is not advantageous for students to merely locate a source; they must use it.

- Determine whether students possess the necessary analysis and synthesis skills to manipulate the information they locate on the Internet, so they can use the sources effectively.

- Be sure that there is both time and support available to conduct the activity effectively.

Furthermore, careful thought must be given to the development of effective activities to assign students as they use those Internet sources. First, as noted earlier, before designing an activity, teachers must consider whether the use of the Internet will enhance student learning. In order to assure this, Harris (1998) stresses that any Internet activity assigned should allow students to do at least one of the following:

- Practice their information-seeking or researching skills

- Increase their knowledge about a topic

- Answer a question they have

- Become acquainted with multiple perspectives on a topic

- Generate and analyze data on a topic

- Solve a real world problem

- Publish information

And, Nelson (2001) stresses that when teachers use the Internet as the basis of their lessons, they are no longer in sole control of the collection, dissemination, and direction of the learning. Instead, now the students access and collect their own information, make the necessary connections, and eventually produce their own end product. Thus, the design of the activity is of crucial importance, and to that end Nelson provides a comprehensive list of guidelines for designing Internet-based activities: Teachers should make sure than an Internet activity

- is linked to specific standards and the curriculum being taught.
- is designed so that students deeply understand the concept being studied.
- can be completed within a reasonable time frame.
- is aligned with the students' prior knowledge.
- is challenging but not frustrating to the students.
- serves a meaningful purpose for the students.
- has an emotional component to motivate students.
- engages students' curiosity.
- allows students the privilege of choice.
- utilizes students' multiple intelligences.
- allows for student collaboration.
- provides immediate feedback.
- fosters reflection.
- includes a variety of assessment possibilities.
- results in a clearly defined end product.

INFORMATIONAL LITERACY

From the coining of the term in 1974 by Paul Zurkowski, information literacy has emerged in the education and information fields as a fundamental literacy for individuals in this century. Today, a number of similar definitions exist; a good one is this: "To be information literate, a person must be able to recognize when information is needed and have the ability to locate, evaluate, and use effectively the needed information" (American Library Association Presidential Committee on Information Literacy, 1989). In effect, information literacy forms the basis for lifelong learning and is common to all disciplines and levels of education. It assists learners in mastering content and expanding their investigations, thus enabling them to become more self-directed and to assume greater control over their learning. An information literate individual is able to

- determine the amount of information required.

- effectively access the information.

- analyze the information and its sources.

- efficiently use the information to achieve a goal. (Association of College and Research Libraries, 2000)

Although it is an independent concept, information literacy, like technology skills, is best taught in close integration with content or subject areas. In addition, according to Harris (1998), there are three basic models through which students can manipulate information literacy effectively. These are the following: (a) interpersonal exchanges, (b) information gathering and analysis, and (c) problem solving. In this text, we will consider only information gathering and analysis, which we will refer to as inquiry-based learning, and problem-solving models, because in the context of the schools we have worked with, interpersonal exchanges cannot often be utilized effectively, since server firewalls usually prevent student access to Web sites that foster interpersonal exchange activities. In addition, most schools also eliminate opportunities for students to access email. Thus, the following sections of this text will examine only activities for inquiry-based learning and problem solving.

INQUIRY-BASED LEARNING

In the past, traditional curricula emphasized teaching and learning based on the student's reading and understanding of a content text. With the influx of new technology, the emphasis has changed, focusing on the student's need to work with multiple resources to learn. The value of inquiry-based learning, which is a student-centered, active-learning approach focusing on questioning, critical thinking, and problem solving, is recognized as a critical component of the changing curriculum (Bruce, 2003). Through the process of inquiry, individuals construct much of their understanding. Inquiry implies a "need or want to know" idea, but it is not so much a seeking of the right answer as a seeking of appropriate solutions to questions and issues. In fact, according to Vacca and Vacca (2008), Internet inquiries broadly follow the elements of the discovery model of investigating a hypothesis or question. They suggest that students follow this process by

1. generating the questions they wish to investigate.

2. searching for the information on the Internet.

3. analyzing the information they have located.

4. compiling the information.

5. sharing the findings with others.

INFORMATION-GATHERING AND ANALYSIS ACTIVITIES

Collaborative Projects

An effective way for students to engage in information-gathering and analysis activities is to participate in collaborative projects. Such collaborative activities involve students from classrooms around the world as they investigate a topic and then share their findings with students in other classrooms through a common Web site. The topics can be as varied as sharing opinions of books read to studying the effects of global warming or predicting the results of a national or international election. Figure 6.1 lists some Web sites that can be used for collaborative projects.

Site	Description
http://eduscapes.com/tap/topic1.htm	The Teacher Tap Web site asks students to solve problems by talking with others, collecting data from remote sites, and sharing the results.
http://k12science2.org/collabprojs. html	The Center for Innovation and Science Education Web site focuses on collaborative projects that utilize real time data available from the Internet and its potential to reach peers and experts around the world. Each project is linked to the National Science Standards and NCTM math standards it supports.
http://www.globalschoolnet.org/	Global SchoolNet's Web site engages students in collaborative projects to develop literacy and communication skills, encourage workforce preparedness, and create multicultural understanding, so they can become productive and effective citizens in an increasingly global economy.
http://mathforum.org/workshops/sum96/data .collections/datalibrary/lesson.ideas.html	This Drexel University Web site offers collaborative problem-solving projects featuring mathematics.
http://www.iearn.org/projects/index.html	The iEARN Web site provides collaborative projects designed to improve the quality of life by asking students to take action as part of what they are learning in the classroom.
http://www.ngcproject.org/	The National Girls Collaborative Project provides opportunities for girls across the world to generate and carry out creative programs and initiatives to create gender equity in the areas of science, technology, engineering, and mathematics.
http://www.hypernews.org/HyperNews/get/www/ collaboration.html	WWW Collaboration Projects provides a comprehensive list of projects that support collaboration by participants.
http://kidlink.org/kidspace/index.php	The kidlink Web site is a kid friendly site that provides a plethora of ways for students to collaborate and network with friends around the world. The collaboration sites are organized by curriculum areas.

Figure 6.1   Web Sites for Collaborative Projects

Electronic Publishing

As we all know, one of the most powerful ways to motivate students to write is to provide an avenue for them to publish what they have written. Electronic publishing allows students to submit their written work to a Web site for peer review by other students, thus creating an interactive venue for students to develop not only their writing skills but their critical reviewing skills as well. Figure 6.2 provides a list of Web sites that facilitate electronic publishing.

Site	Description
http://www.airnyc.org/info/Young-Writers-Clubhouse-268067.html	The Young Writers Club urges students to learn about great authors and then emulate them by composing their own writings for submission.
http://www.realkids.com/club.shtml	Deborah Morris, a real author, provides students an opportunity to learn about writing first hand and then share their own writing with peers for a critical review.
http://teacher.scholastic.com/writewit/poetry/index.htm	This Web site, sponsored by Scholastic.com provides opportunities for students to e-mail their work to professional writers, who will comment on it.
http://www.amphi.com/~pgreenle/EEI/studentpublish.html	This Web site lists a plethora of other Web sites that facilitate student publishing.
http://teacher.scholastic.com/writewit/index.htm	This Web site accepts students' written poetry that is 20 lines or less in length. Poets 18 and younger compete for $1,000 in monthly prizes.
http://www.thestarlitecafe.com/	The Starlite Café Web site invites writers of all ages to submit their poetry and provides an opportunity to choose the color, font, and background for their work as well as to create an online portfolio of what they have written. In addition, writers may choose to let readers rate their writing. Links to other Web publishing sites are provided as well.
http://www.publishingstudents.com/	This is a site for teachers, librarians, parents, and students interested in publishing students' writing. It contains writing by students and advice by teachers and professionals about publishing students' work.
http://englishonline.tki.org.nz/	Writer Window is a Web site primarily for writers 17 and younger. It publishes stories, poems, and research as well as TV and movie reviews and provides students from all over the world an opportunity to help one another improve their writing.

Figure 6.2   Web Sites for Internet Publishing

Virtual Field Trips

In this day of tight school budgets and high-stakes testing, opportunities for field trips, especially in middle and high schools, seem to be on the decline. However, one cannot deny the value of field trips, for they provide students with expanded learning experiences. One way to facilitate the field trip experience without taking students out of the classroom or using tightly budgeted funds is to initiate a virtual field trip using the Internet.

However, before one launches a virtual field trip, Nelson (2001) stresses that teachers must ask themselves how the planned virtual field trip can be connected to the curriculum, warning that the trips cannot merely be an experience but must, instead, increase the students' knowledge of a concept they are studying. In other words, teachers must have direct goals and objectives in mind for what they want students to learn as well as specific end products they will expect students to produce as a result of their virtual adventure to a new and exciting place. The site http://www.campsilos.org/excursions/hc/fieldtrip.htm, developed by Internet4Classrooms and designed to help teachers use the Internet effectively, provides a comprehensive template entitled *Why Take Field Trips* on how to plan for a virtual field trip. Information is provided on (1) trip selection, (2) logistics planning, (3) preparing students for the trip, (4) final planning, (5) conducting the trip, (6) activities that will occur during the trip, (7) post–field trip activities, and (8) evaluating the trip. Figure 6.3 provides a list of Web sites that offer additional information about virtual field trips.

Site	Description
http://www.field-trips.org/vft/index.htm	The Tramline Web site provides annotated trips to a variety of sites on science, literature, social studies, and other topics. The site includes trip introductions and resources for teachers to use to set the stage for the trips.
http://www.vickiblackwell.com/vft.html	This Web site provides a plethora of teacher-tested virtual field trips.
http://eduscapes.com/tap/topic35.htm	The Teacher Tap Web site answers questions about what kinds of virtual field trips are available online, what trips teachers can explore with their students, and how to integrate virtual field trips into the classroom routine.
http://www.uen.org/utahlink/tours/	This Web site, sponsored by the Utah Education Network, provides resources for taking a virtual field trip as well as creating one's own virtual field trip and visiting other sites related to virtual field trips.
http://www.techtrekers.com/virtualft.htm	TechTrekers offers a comprehensive list of virtual field trips.
http://www.internet4classrooms.com/vft.htm	The Internet4Classrooms Web site provides a variety of virtual field trip opportunities as well as articles to help teachers plan for an effective virtual field trip.
http://www.kn.pacbell.com/wired/vidconf/adventures.html	The AT&T education Web site provides a comprehensive listing of virtual field trips as well as interactive videoconferencing, which allows students and teachers to see and hear each other simultaneously across the state or around the world.
http://atozkids.com/trip.html	The A–Z Kidstuff Web site provides a list of virtual field trips for students of all ages.

Figure 6.3   Web Sites for Virtual Field Trips

WebQuests

The WebQuest is an inquiry-based lesson format, first developed by Bernie Dodge of San Diego State University with input from Tom March, a San Diego State University/Pacific Bell fellow in 1995. In effect, WebQuests are an intriguing and effective model for engaging students as they use the Internet to study and understand complex subjects. Overall, WebQuests resemble typical informational inquiry models and are usually composed of seven basic components. Sheryl Sejnost (personal communication, October 7, 2008), a middle school special education teacher, offers this take on the seven steps:

1. The **introduction** establishes the learners' place in a hypothetical situation, such as, "You are living in New York in _____. Every day you see a boatload of immigrants arriving from many countries. You wonder who they are, where they come from, and what will they do in America.

2. Next, students are assigned **a role or a purpose** for engaging in the task that they are assigned, such as, "You are a historical detective in New York City."

3. Students then proceed to complete a **task,** which might look like this: "Your task is to determine which American immigrant has had the greatest influence on American life."

4. At this point, students are ready to follow a **process** to complete the task, which might look like this: "Your group will choose one immigrant from each of the following catagories: science, math, medicine, sports, entertainment, humanities, arts, politics, and business to research using the Web sites listed in the resources section."

5. The specific Web sites that students can refer to are then listed in the **resources** section.

6. Directions and requirements for the task are listed in the **guidance** section.

7. Finally, in the **conclusion,** students report what they have learned and are given opportunities for further analysis of their topic.

The real effectiveness of WebQuests lies in the fact that students do not spend huge amounts of time surfing the Internet searching for information but rather access information immediately by searching preselected sites; this gives them more time to analyze, synthesize, and evaluate the information they have found to address high-level questions and alternative perspectives. Figure 6.4 is a list of Web sites that provide information on how to develop WebQuests, how to evaluate WebQuests, and where to find effective WebQuests for students to participate in.

Site	Description
http://www.webquest.org/index-create.php	Bernie Dodge, the creator of WebQuests, maintains this Web site, which provides current and complete information about the WebQuest model. This site presents a plethora of resources previously linked to the WebQuest Page at San Diego State University as well as those at the portal at WebQuest.org. It gives instructions on how to create WebQuests and how to evaluate them as well as a comprehensive listing of completed WebQuests.
http://www.vickiblackwell.com/webquests.html	This Web site provides a plethora of teacher-tested WebQuests.
http://eduscapes.com/tap/topic4.htm	The Teacher Tap Web site provides answers to what a WebQuest is as well as information about where WebQuests for specific content areas can be found.
http://school.discoveryeducation.com/schrockguide/webquest/webquest.html	Developed by Kathy Schrock, this Web site provides a comprehensive list of effective WebQuests for classroom use.
http://bestwebquests.com/	Tom March, who was instrumental in assisting Bernie Dodge in developing the concept of WebQuests, presents current information on WebQuests and evaluates current WebQuests to determine which are best.
http://www.teachnology.com/teachers/lesson_plans/computing/web_quests/	This comprehensive Web site provides information on how to create a WebQuest, presents a draft rubric for evaluating WebQuests, and offers a huge directory of available WebQuests for student use.
http://www.teachersfirst.com/summer/webquest/quest-a.shtml	Web Quest 101 provides a tutorial to introduce you to WebQuests and leads you step by step through a creation of a WebQuest.
http://www.teacherweb.com/	The TeacherWeb site provides a list of links to locate a WebQuest and tips to help you create your own.

Figure 6.4   Web Sites for WebQuests

PROBLEM-BASED PROJECT LEARNING

In the early 1970s, McMaster University, located in Hamilton, Ontario, Canada, introduced problem-based learning in medical education, an approach that would eventually influence university teaching and learning dynamics in many universities throughout the world (Stepien & Gallagher, 1993). Problem-based learning (PBL) is an instructional strategy characterized by the use of real world problems as a context for students to learn critical thinking and problem-solving skills and to acquire knowledge of the essential concepts of a course. Often, however, the problems presented are complex and may not result in an obvious, easy-to-locate solution. But, when students use PBL, they engage in relevant and meaningful inquiry, thus acquiring lifelong learning skills, which include the ability to find and use appropriate learning resources. Thus, for the purpose of this text, we will combine the concepts of problem-based learning and project learning into a single category, problem-based project learning. The following sections of this text provide a brief discussion of a suggested process for using both problem-based learning and project-based learning.

A Process for Using Problem-Based Project Learning

Fogarty (1997) sets forth a clear set of steps that help guide us in conducting problem-based learning. They are as follows:

1. Meet the problem: Students are introduced to the problem through a case study or a scenario.

2. Define the problem: Students determine exactly what the problem is, state it in their own words, and clarify what they know and what they need to know in order to solve the problem.

3. Gather the facts.

4. Establish a hypothesis.

5. Conduct research to accrue more data and information.

6. Rephrase the problem: Students restate their original hypothesis to include newly discovered information, thus making their approach more specific.

7. Generate alternatives: Students offer solutions and alternative solutions.

8. Advocate the solution: Students justify their solutions and ultimately choose the best solution.

To put Fogarty's steps into practice, students are given an ill-structured problem that is usually presented in a scenario or case study format. They assume the role of a doctor, scientist, historian, or other individual who has a stake in the problem, and they work in small groups to discuss their ideas related to the problem in an attempt to define the broad nature of the problem. Throughout this discussion, students pose questions on features of the problem they do not understand. These questions are recorded by the group to help define what they know, and more important, what they do not know. Next, students rank, in order of importance, the questions generated in the session to determine which ones to research; they also discuss what resources will be needed to find the answers. After students conduct research individually on these questions, they reconvene, discuss their findings, connect new concepts to old ones, and continue to define new learning issues as they progress through the problem. Finally, students present their solution(s) to the class.

Social Action Projects

Social action projects revolve around important global, social, economic, political, and environmental issues that students research, such as global warming, endangered animals, ozone depletion, homelessness, gender equality, air pollution, water pollution, human rights, etc. The I-Search model is an excellent activity for students to use to investigate social action projects.

I-Search Project

The I-Search project (Macrorie, 1988) encourages students to investigate a topic they are curious about or interested in by following a different path than that of the usual research paper format. In this alternative to the traditional research project (which often results in students merely recopying the words of their sources), students can research by visiting places relevant to the topic, interviewing experts on the topic or in the field, and conducting Internet searches. Alejandro (1989) suggests that this strategy is especially effective for English language learners, since it allows them to focus on topics that may already be familiar to them. One could assume, then, that the same would hold true for special education students.

Steps for Conducting the I-Search Project

1. First, students choose a topic that interests them. Tierney and Readence (2005) stress that few limits should be placed on topic choice so that students can choose a topic that will truly engage them and sustain their interest.

2. Next, Macrorie suggests that, when students have chosen their topics, they not only share the topics but also clarify what led them to that topic choice, thus not only allowing students to share their own personal knowledge of and interest in the various topics but also providing both basic knowledge and help to others as they begin their searches.

3. Once topics have been chosen, students formulate a plan of action to carry out their research. Macrorie provides the following suggestions:

   a. First, students must determine who are the experts on their chosen topic and which sources are the best to utilize.

   b. Next, students must prepare themselves by reading about the topic so that they create questions to guide their information searches.

   c. Then students should plan to interview an expert; they should first determine an appropriate format for the interview, such as whether they should take notes or use an audio recorder or video camera to record pertinent information.

   d. When the interview is complete, students validate the information they received with comparable information gleaned from other resources, such as secondary sources.

4. Finally, students are ready to tell the story of their research project, making it as personal as possible by including information about why they chose their topic, what they learned about their topic, what special experiences they had as they did their research, and what they learned from conducting their research.

5. The I-Search paper concludes with a list of sources, including the names of the experts interviewed.

Conley (2008) offers yet another option on the I-Search project by suggesting that the final product developed by students can be more than just a written paper. Instead, students may choose to develop a Web page, institute a blog, create a podcast, or engage in other such creative projects. See Figure 6.5 for an I-Search project assignment and Figure 6.6 for a rubric for an I-Search project.

I-Search Project

Objectives:

1. Conduct an information inquiry using a variety of sources to investigate a problem or issue from one of the following perspectives: (a) cause-effect, (b) problem-solution, or (c) comparison-contrast.

2. Use a software program to publish the research findings in one of the following forms: pamphlet, PowerPoint presentation, or graphic representation.

Assignment Requirements: At least three to five sources should be consulted. Those sources starred below are required.

1. Books* such as reference books, maps, atlases, encyclopedia

2. Periodicals

3. Newspapers

4. The Internet*

5. Personal interviews

Possible Topic Choices: (If you choose another topic, have it approved by the teacher.)

Alcohol abuse	Death penalty	Human rights
Animal abuse	Discrimination	Immigration
Anorexia	Drug addiction	Pollution
Bioengineered foods	Endangered species	Poverty
Bulimia	Global warming	Smoking
Childhood obesity	Gun control	Video games
Crime prevention	Homelessness	

Figure 6.5   I-Search Project Assignment Sheet

Element	1	2	3	4	5
Issue and Support	Problem not clearly stated	Problem clearly stated with 4 or fewer facts, statistics	Problem clearly stated with 5–8 facts, statistics	Problem clearly stated with 8–10 facts, statistics	Problem clearly stated with 10 or more facts, statistics
Research	No evidence of scholarly research	Scholarly research with 0–2 sources; required sources not used	Scholarly research with 3–4 sources; required sources used	Scholarly research with 5 sources; required sources used	Scholarly research with 5 or more sources; required sources used
Organization	Chronology of problem not provided	Chronology of problem briefly provided	Chronology of problem summarized generally	Chronology of problem clearly described	Chronology of problem described in detail
Issue	Cause-effect, problem-solution, or comparison-contrast elements not provided	Cause-effect, problem-solution, or comparison-contrast elements briefly provided	Cause-effect, problem-solution, or comparison-contrast summarized in general terms	Cause-effect, problem-solution, or comparison-contrast clearly described	Cause-effect, problem-solution, or comparison-contrast clearly described in detail
Appearance	Assignment not developed using appropriate software	Assignment developed using appropriate software; careless	Assignment developed using appropriate software; neat and clear	Assignment developed using appropriate software; neat, clear, attractive	Assignment developed using appropriate software; neat, clear, attractive, creative
Mechanics	Assignment has many grammatical errors	Assignment has several grammatical errors	Assignment has some grammatical errors	Assignment has minimal grammatical errors	Assignment has no grammatical errors
Elements	Assignment has all elements missing	Assignment has most elements missing	Assignment has few elements missing	Assignment has 1 element missing	Assignment has no elements missing

Figure 6.6   I-Search Rubric

PROJECT-BASED LEARNING

Project-based learning is similar to problem-based learning because it is centered on the learner and directs students to investigate a problem, issue, or topic of interest related to real-world concerns; however, this model typically begins with a product, performance, or presentation in mind that requires specific content area skills (Newell, 2003). In effect, students should do the following: (1) identify a purpose for creating a product and a specific audience at whom the product is aimed; (2) use multiple resources to investigate their ideas, apply the information, and create a design for their product; and, finally, (3) present their project to the class. Often, project-based learning requires the use of presentation software programs such as Microsoft's PowerPoint or video clips.

For successful project-based learning, Roblyer (2003) suggests that students adhere to the following process:

1. Conduct research on the chosen topic in order to locate materials, analyze data, and summarize findings.

2. Develop a storyboard as an outline for the project. Roblyer (2003) suggests that this can be easily accomplished by using index cards or sticky notes to depict each frame of the planned presentation.

3. Create each frame of the presentation.

4. Insert graphs, video clips, animations, and clip art into frames as needed.

5. Add links or script to the frames as needed.

6. Test the final product, and revise it as necessary.

Finally, of course, if students utilize specific presentation software, they must receive instruction on how to use it. The project assignment presented in Figure 6.7 and the rubric presented in Figure 6.8 were created by Sheryl Sejnost for use in a middle school social studies class as part of their study of World War II (S. Sejnost, personal communication, October 7, 2008).

World War II Project Requirements

To complete your study of World War II, you and a partner will create a PowerPoint presentation to explain the importance of a topic from World War II. Your project will focus on presenting all of the important facts about this topic by including the following:

- A PowerPoint presentation that contains a title slide, at least 10 additional slides that identify your topic and explain its significance to World War II, and a bibliography slide that includes information for all facts, pictures, video clips, and recordings included in your presentation
- At least two video clips that are appropriate for your topic
- At least three pictures, with audio recordings, that show the significance of your chosen event to World War II

As you develop your presentation, be sure to

- complete a storyboard to plan out your PowerPoint before creating the project.
- use appropriate elements such as font, color, graphics, clip art, transitions, etc.

Finally, each day you will complete a daily log to document the work you completed and a goal for the next day.

Possible topics include the following:

Important People	Navajo code talkers	**The Holocaust**
Stalin	Tuskegee Airmen	Auschwitz
Mussolini	paratroopers in France	Anne Frank
Hitler	Battle of Midway	human experiments
Churchill	Battle of the Bulge	in the camps
Eisenhower	D-Day	life in the camps
MacArthur	Bataan Death March	
	kamikaze	**U.S. Front**
War	Allies and Axis	victory garden
Pearl Harbor	Nuremberg trials	jobs for women
the atomic bomb	Iwo Jima	Japanese internment camp
Doolittle raid	V-E Day	war bonds
blitzkrieg		war factories in the U.S.

Figure 6.7   World War II Project Assignment

SOURCE: Developed by Sheryl Sejnost, Mannheim Middle School, Melrose Park, IL.

Names _____ Topic _____

Category	Points	Excellent: 4 points	Good: 3 points	Fair: 2 points	Poor: 1 point
Storyboard		Storyboard is complete with many details and complete script.	Storyboard is complete with some details and incomplete script.	Storyboard is incomplete with few details and incomplete script.	Storyboard is incomplete with no details and no script.
Daily Log		Daily Log is complete with many details and complete goals.	Daily Log is complete with some details and few goals.	Daily Log is incomplete with few details and few goals.	Daily Log is incomplete with no details and missing goals.
Content		Information is correct, relevant, and presented in small phrases.	Information is correct, mostly relevant, and presented in small phrases.	Information is somewhat correct, relevant, and presented in small phrases.	Information is incorrect, irrelevant, and not presented in small phrases.
Video		Video is relevant, interesting, and integrated well into the presentation.	Video is somewhat relevant and fit into the presentation.	Video is somewhat irrelevant and not integrated into the presentation well.	Video is irrelevant and not integrated into the presentation.
Narration		Audio clip is narrated clearly, and the information is very significant.	Audio clip is clear and the information is significant.	Audio clip is difficult to hear, and the information isn't very significant.	Audio clip is not present.
Picture		Picture is very interesting and conveys a great deal of information about the topic.	Picture is somewhat interesting and conveys information about the topic.	Picture is not very interesting and has little information about the topic.	Picture has little to do with the topic.
Bibliography		All sources are cited correctly.	Most sources are cited correctly.	Some sources are cited correctly.	No sources are cited correctly.
PowerPoint Elements		The background, font, transitions, etc. are creative and interesting.	The background, font, transitions, etc. are appropriate.	The background, font, transitions, etc. are somewhat distracting.	The background, font, transitions, etc. are not appropriate.
Oral Presentation		The presentation is fluent from the beginning to the end.	The presentation is somewhat fluent from the beginning to the end.	The presentation is not fluent from the beginning to the end.	The presentation is difficult to follow.

Figure 6.8   World War II Project Rubric

SOURCE: Developed by Sheryl Sejnost, Mannheim Middle School, Melrose Park, IL.

Historical Inquiry

In every discipline, students must be taught to think in a way that is appropriate to that discipline. In other words, they must be able to read science material like scientists; mathematical material like mathematicians; English like authors and poets; and history like historians. Roblyer (2003) suggests that the way to accomplish this is to develop the critical reading skills practiced by experts in these fields. In addition, he posits that to facilitate the development of these skills, students must have access to the study of primary source documents, and he describes the GATHER strategy as developed by teachers who worked on a project developed by the Center for Electronic Studying at the University of Oregon. The GATHER strategy is specifically designed for historical inquiry using a Web-based environment and is made up of six basic steps, which guide students along the path of conducting research in the same way that historians of any discipline do. These steps are as follows:

1. **G**et an overview.
2. **A**sk a probing question.
3. **T**riangulate the data.
4. **H**ypothesize a tentative answer.
5. **E**xplore and interpret the data.
6. **R**ecord and support the conclusions. (Roblyer, 2003, p. 247)

Digital Storytelling

As we all know, storytelling is an age-old tradition and was probably the first teaching tool ever used. When our civilization was in its earliest stages, it was through the oral tradition of storytelling that the young learned what they needed to know to become healthy, productive adults. Even today people of all ages enjoy a good story; isn't that why we are intrigued with a good book or an intriguing movie or television show? They all tell a story!

Today the revered tradition of storytelling has been brought into the technological age through the use of digital storytelling. In this technological activity, computer-based tools, such as graphic images, text, recorded audio narration, video clips, and music are used to present us with a specific topic discussed from a particular point of view. Digital stories, like any story, can vary in length, but most such stories developed for use in classrooms are about two to ten minutes in length. They can deal with any subject, from personal accounts to the recounting of historical events, ecological movements, or social issues. Above all, in digital storytelling, students are encouraged to take a clear, close look at the content, topic, or event to be featured in order to clarify their own thinking about it and their understanding of it. In truth, an effective digital story goes beyond a mere reporting of facts and statistics and, like all good stories, includes a personal understanding or reflection about the moral or the lesson the story has taught.

The Web site DigiTales (*Seven Steps to Create a DigiTales Story,* 2004) suggests that to write a digital story, students move through a series of four production steps which, in turn, contain seven process steps. These are the following:

I. Preproduction: Find and organize the idea.

Step 1: Develop the script: In this step, students must strive to script the story they wish to tell from their own specific perspective. The script should be tightly woven to include exactly what media enhancements such as video clips, music, graphics, etc. will best present not only the information but the author's message as well. This phase may well take from 30% to 40% of the time devoted to the entire assignment.

Step 2: Plan the project: This step of the project mimics the outline portion of essay writing. However, rather than adhering to the usual outline format, digital storytellers often use a storyboard template, which is a graphic organizer that allows students to visualize the details of all aspects of their story, its narration, images, titles, transitions, special effects, music, etc.

Step 3: Organize the folders: This step allows students to manage the various computer files, such as text, images, sound, and music that will be used in the digital story.

II. Production: Gather and prepare the digital media.

Step 4: Record the voiceover: This step focuses on creating the script's voiceover as well as recording digital interviews. Students should be encouraged to choose vocal presentations that reflect emotional tones rather than mere dry recitation.

Step 5: In this step, students gather the media they will use and then edit the images, sound, and music in order to convey the message they are sending through the digital story they are telling. In order to accomplish this, students should be encouraged to exercise their creativity by using special effects and appropriate music. However, be sure to caution students to use all sources legally and ethically by following copyright guidelines and providing appropriate references.

III. Postproduction: Put the story together.

Step 6: Create the first and last versions: This is the step where students must first view their digital story in its rough version. After viewing the flow of the first version of the story, students then decide if they need to add, edit, or cut anything. Once this is done, students are ready to fine tune their digital story and prepare the final version.

Lesson Title	**Welcome to Ellis Island Digital Story**
Subject Areas	Language arts and social studies
Purpose of Lesson	Help students better understand and communicate what life was like for an immigrant entering the United States through Ellis Island
Time Required	1 week
Student Activities	Research immigration through Ellis Island during the 1890s
	Use this research to put together a digital story, using iMovie, of an immigrant from a country of student's choice
	Compress movie into QuickTime to share with class
Illinois Learning Standards	Social studies—16A, 17C, 18A, 18B, 18C
	Language—5A, 5B, 5C
Learning Strategy	Question-answer relationships using "in my head" questions
Differentiated Instruction	Differentiated according to interest and readiness
National Education Technology Standards	Creativity and innovation
	Communication and collaboration
	Research and information fluency
	Critical thinking, problem solving, and decision making
	Digital citizenship
	Technology operation and concepts
Lesson Procedures	Students will use different resources, including but not limited to books, the Internet, United Streaming video, audio, and primary sources to research immigration through Ellis Island in the 1890s.
	Students will complete a storyboard of a personal narrative of the Ellis Island experience to be used for planning the digital story.
	Students will use primary sources, narration, and video to create a digital story using iMovie to communicate what they inferred about life for an immigrant.
Resources	Learning links for immigration: http://www.d83.org/SocStud/immigration.html
	American Memory historical collections: http://memory.loc.gov/
	http://teacher.scholastic.com/activities/immigration/
	http://ellisisland.org/
	http://www.42explore2.com/migration.htm
	http://memory.loc.gov/ammem/index.html
Assessment	Rubric
Comments	This activity uses visual literacy to give students a deeper understanding of immigration through Ellis Island and what the immigrants experienced. It is also a creative way for students to write a personal narrative. It can also be used as a form of assessment of the students' understanding of the Ellis Island experience.

Figure 6.9   Assignment for Digital Storytelling

SOURCE: Developed by Sheila Ruh, Mannheim Middle School, Melrose Park, IL.

IV. Distribution: Share the story.

Step 7: Applause: This step is where students share their digital story with others. They can make DVDs; post the story on school, community, or personal Web sites; and, of course, share it at educational conferences.

See Figure 6.9 for a suggestion for digital storytelling assignment and Figure 6.10 for a rubric to assess a digital story. Figure 6.11 provides a list of Web sites for digital storytelling.

Criteria	3 Points	2 Points	1 Point	0 Points
Creativity	Very creative and an excellent use of critical thinking skills	Somewhat creative and a good use of critical thinking skills	Not very creative and little use of critical thinking skills	Not creative and no use of critical thinking skills
Storyboard	Detailed planning, including a script, drawings, and appropriate sequencing	Some planning with a few drawings, a brief script, and some sequencing	Little planning with one drawing, a few phrases, and little sequencing	No planning with no drawings, no script, and no sequencing
Content	Content is accurate, and relevant and tells an excellent story	Content is accurate, and somewhat relevant and tells a story	Content is not completely accurate, not very relevant, and unclear	Content is neither accurate nor relevant and does not tell a story
Images	Excellent use of images that are realistic and visually enhance the story	Good use of images that are somewhat realistic and enhance the story	Images are not realistic and do not enhance the story	No images used in the project
Editing	All transitions, audio, and effects add to overall continuity of the presentation	Most transitions, audio, and effects add to overall continuity of the presentation	Some transitions, audio, and effects add to overall continuity of the presentation	Transitions, audio, and effects do not add to overall continuity of the presentation
Timeliness	The project was turned in at the beginning of class	The project was turned in at the end of class	The project was turned in one day late	The project was turned in two or more days late
Documentation	All sources cited; correct format used in bibliography	Most sources cited; correct format used in bibliography	Some sources cited; correct format used in bibliography	No sources cited and correct format not used in bibliography
Collaboration	All members of group worked together equally	Most members of group worked together equally	Some members of group worked together equally	Group did not work together at all

Figure 6.10   Rubric for Digital Storytelling

SOURCE: Developed by Sheila Ruh, Mannheim Middle School, Melrose Park, IL.

Site	Description
http://teachingteachers.com/	This Web site provides information on how to create digital stories as well as tutorials and answers to frequently asked questions about digital storytelling.
http://www.teachingteacher.com/	This Web site features information on the power of digital storytelling as well as reasons for implementing storytelling in the classroom and links to other sites that can help students learn how to use digital storytelling in the classroom.
http://www.storycenter.org/	Developed by the Center for Digital Storytelling, this Web site provides assistance for using the various tools of digital media to create a story.
http://techteachers.com/?s=story+telling	Developed by Meg Ormiston, this Web site provides a collection of resources to help educators explore and utilize the tools needed to create digital stories.
http://www.jakesonline.org/storytelling.htm	This Web site offers links to (1) articles and resources about the process of digital storytelling, (2) visual literacy resources such as storyboards, and (3) articles about digital storytelling.
http://www.adobe.com/education/instruction/adsc/	This Web site, maintained by Adobe, presents a plethora of resources for teachers, such as introductions to digital photography and video, other digital media tips, training tips, and lessons and activities to help teachers and students create digital stories.
http://digitalstoryteller.org	Digital Storyteller is a Web-based tool that presents teachers and students with easy access to digital images and materials to help them create and develop digital stories.
http://www.shambles.net/pages/staff/dstorytell/	This Web site provides a plethora of links to a variety of sources to help teachers and students create effective digital stories.

Figure 6.11   Web Sites for Digital Storytelling

MEDIA LITERACY

The media, which include newspapers, magazines, radio, television, movies, music, video games, and the Internet, are collectively an instrumental force in influencing peoples' perception of the world and the way they think and believe. In fact, students come into the classroom with knowledge, ideas, prejudices, and experiences related to what they have discovered from the media. Thus, media literacy is certainly one of the new literacies of the 21st century. According to the National Association for Media Literacy Education (2008), media literacy is a series of abilities to access, analyze, evaluate, and communicate different forms of information. Sharrer (2003) reminds us that media literacy means students can critically analyze what they see and read and, as a result, are able to understand and appreciate the effects the media has on its viewers. Yet, while children are able to listen, read, and understand basic ideas and symbols in the media, they need to develop their skills in order to acquire a critical perspective. However, media messages are not always what they seem to be; they often have multidimensional purposes (Potter, 2001). If people do not pay attention to the messages, the media are in control, and their messages are accepted, including bias from articles and advertising. Unrau (2008) consolidates the core principles of media literacy by presenting the work of Considine and Haley (1999), McBrien (2005), and Thomas and Jollis (2005), who remind us of the following:

- All media and their messages are constructed.
- Every medium utilizes its own language and techniques.
- The audience constructs its own interpretation of media messages.
- Media, with [their] forms and rules of construction, transmit values and ideologies.
- Media messages have political, economic, social, and cultural consequences. (Unrau, 2008, p. 271)

And, on the basis of the above principles, Unrau (2008) suggests that we need to remind students to consider

- what the source of the message is and who created it, because that will help students determine what was put in the message and what was left out as well as how the message correlates with other messages.
- what techniques and strategies have contributed to the construction of the message, because the media's use of imagery, sound, and symbols not only enables students to better understand and appreciate the message but also make them aware of possible manipulation.
- how the message can be interpreted in alternative ways, because, after all, we each perceive what we see and hear through our own lenses, so it is important to realize such differing perceptions and interpretations and seek to determine whether they have merit, validity, and justification.
- what values and perspectives the message transmits and whose values and perspectives are being transmitted, because sometimes a latent message or subtext is buried within the more overt message sent, and students need to be made aware of that.
- what social, political, economic, and/or cultural action the message urges, and in whose interest the message has been sent, because students need to be able to determine if they have been given the truth or if the message has been designed to manipulate them.

The following sections focus on a variety of activities that will help students develop their media literacy.

Newspapers and Magazines

Newspaper and magazine circulation has diminished today, because many consumers listen to or watch the news on radio, television, or the Internet. Because they only listen to or watch the news, students do not understand news topics in depth; they form opinions based on words or pictures. Using the myriad of classroom activities below, teachers can use newspapers and magazines to help students become better readers.

1. Find the main idea of an article by identifying the five Ws (who, what, when, where, and why).

2. Cut out two different articles, for example a sports article and a news article. Have the students compare and contrast the style and content of the two articles.

3. Make a budget to buy groceries for a family of four people. Look at grocery ads and select items for a week's menu. Write down the price for each item and tabulate the results. See if your grocery list fits your budget.

4. Look for articles that relate to issues that students read about in class. Ask students to compare the content of these articles with what they read about these issues in their textbooks, and have them consider ways to address these issues.

5. Cut up an article, and put the pieces in an envelope. Have students put the pieces together in the right order.

6. Cut out headlines from several newspapers. Have students write articles that fit the headlines. Compare their answers with the original ones.

7. Cut out pictures from a newspaper. Have students create their own headlines or articles from the pictures.

8. Get two newspapers, and find a news story that both cover. Cut the stories out, and have students look for bias in both versions.

9. Ask students to read two different articles in the newspaper. Have them list five important bullet points for each article. They should be prepared to share their answers with a partner, a small group, or the class.

10. Read the weather report for one week. Keep track of the predictions, and determine how many were correct.

11. Conduct a newspaper project. See Figure 6.12 for an example of a newspaper project for social studies.

Assignment: Create the front page of a newspaper focusing on a particular era in history, like the Middle Ages, or on a literary work. Include specific references from the text. Be creative with clip art, fonts, pictures, story ideas, etc.

Group Grade	50 Points Possible	
	Creative title of newspaper (include date and year)	_____ /3 points
	Use newspaper format	_____ /2 points
	Include an ad	_____ /5 points
	Include one of the following	_____ /5 points
	1. a five frame comic strip	
	2. two help-wanted ads	
	3. two obituaries	
	Creativity; accuracy to the text	_____ /10 points

Each person in the group must choose **one** of the following assignments:

1. **News Story**

   Write a headline and a byline.

   Write a three-paragraph story about a character or event in the text.

   Begin the story with the most important information.

   Answer the questions of who, what, when, where, and why. _____ /25 points

2. **Write Two Dear_____ Letters**

   Create a byline.

   Each letter must be at least a half page in length and relate to a problem in the text.

   Write an answer for each problem. _____ /25 points

3. **Feature Article**

   Write a headline and a byline

   Write one page providing detailed information about an idea, situation, or event.

   Focus on human interest.

   Use anecdotes and quotes to tell the story. _____ /25 points

4. **Editorial**

   Write a headline and a byline.

   Write a one-page editorial, stating an opinion about an issue in the text.

   Use clear details to support your view. _____ /25 points

5. **Sports Story**

   Write a headline and a byline.

   Write a three-paragraph story about a sporting event during the time period.

   Begin the story with the most important question.

   Answer the questions of who was involved (team), what happened (score),

   and when and where the event took place. _____ /25 points

Figure 6.12   Newspaper Project Assignment

Advertisements

Newspaper or magazine ads are a good source to use to help students identify persuasive techniques and the elements of faulty logic. The assignment detailed in Figure 6.13 helps students evaluate the advertisements they see in magazines, in newspapers, and on television. Before asking the students to complete the assignment, be sure to introduce the various propaganda techniques shown in Figure 6.14.

Steps for Evaluating Print Advertisements

1. Distribute ads from newspapers or magazines, or ask students to find ads.

2. Students can work with a partner or a small group to identify the following information:

   a. Who is selling the product?

   b. Who is the intended audience?

   c. What "loaded" words are used in the ad?

   d. What does the ad promise?

   e. What visual details promote the product?

   f. What propaganda techniques are used?

3. Have students share their answers with small groups or with the whole class.

4. Create a follow-up activity. For example, give a quiz, or have students write an ad or present a commercial.

Figure 6.13   Evaluating Advertisements Assignment

Technique	Example
Bandwagon	Buy Brand X jeans so you are not set apart from the crowd.
Testimonial	Celebrities endorse the item.
Emotional Appeal	Buy this cereal. It has all the vitamins to keep your child healthy.
False Cause and Effect	This product will make you look years younger.
Name Calling	You might be a loser if you do not use this product.

Figure 6.14   Examples of Propaganda Techniques

Editorials

Roe, Stoodt-Hill, and Burns (2007) tell us that editorials are a form of exposition that students can use to convey information from a particular point of view. Since the purpose of an editorial is to try to convince the reader to accept the author's argument on an issue, writing editorials is an excellent way to practice writing the persuasive essay, a skill students are often asked to perform on standardized tests like the ACT.

In order to facilitate student writing of an editorial, Roe et al. (2007) suggest that students be able to identify the following in any expository composition:

- Author's purpose
- Author's argument
- Details and their sequence as used by the author to support the argument
- Organizational pattern
- Any bias related either to the topic or the audience

When students are ready to write an editorial, these are a few steps they can follow:

1. Choose an issue or a problem.
2. Carefully research the problem, looking at both sides of the issue.
3. State your position on or solution to the issue.
4. State reasons, facts, and examples to support your chosen position.
5. Explain the other side to the issue, and present reasons, facts, and examples that focus on its weaknesses.
6. Restate the position you have taken.
7. Use controlled, moderate language and strong, logical arguments to express the reasons, facts, and examples in your editorial.

News Broadcasts

Radio and television broadcast the news everyday. The format of nightly news is good for reviewing content, analyzing material, and promoting listening and speaking skills. Teachers can ask students to listen to or watch the nightly news and make a list of the kinds of features on the program. The features they discern can then be woven into an assignment based on a specific content area.

In order to do this, design an assignment to focus on incidents in history, on a novel or play, or on a famous scientist, mathematician, artist, or author. Give students part of a class period to choose the groups they will work in, determine their roles, decide the order of items in the broadcast, and choose specific stories or topics. Then, one full class period should be devoted to allowing students to write their scripts. Figure 6.15 provides detailed guidelines for this assignment.

News Broadcast

Assignment: Your job is to create a news program based on incidents in Acts I and II of *Macbeth*. Work together as a team, and cover information from your reading. Mimic broadcasts that are on the radio or television. Remember, you only know as much as the characters in the play know. Be creative!

Roles:

Two Coanchors: Report on the story that took place in the play. Remember, an anchor is unbiased and reports only on the facts.

Interviewer and Interviewee: Interview a character from the play. The person can be a major character such as Macbeth or Banquo or a minor character like the porter. Each person should write five questions and answers; choose the questions together so their order is logical.

Meteorologist: Report on the weather that occurs in the play. Pay close attention to act 1 scene 3, act 2 scene 3, and act 2 scene 4.

Analyst: Give an editorial on the events in the play. Discuss an area of concern, and include your opinion.

Scripts:

Each of you will need to type out his or her own script, including transitions between segments. Each script should be at least three-quarters of a page in length (double-spaced, 12-point type). Be sure to put your name on the script. Interviewers and interviewees will need copies of their scripts for their partners to read off of during the presentation.

Presentation:

You will receive a grade for your presentation. On the day your group presents, please turn in a sheet of paper with the grading criteria shown below and your names and roles written on it. If you are absent the day of the presentation, you need to make a cover for your script that includes a title, an illustration that represents the ideas in the script, and two relevant quotations from the play that relate to the script.

Grading Criteria
Presentation:
  Clear, audible
  Good pace
  Polished delivery   _____ /10 points
Script:
  Proper margins and fonts
  Adequate length
  Relates directly to the play
  Has a good story line   _____ /20 points

Figure 6.15   News Broadcast Project Assignment for English

VISUAL LITERACY

Infants do not have the ability to verbalize their thoughts; however, they have the basic skills of visual literacy, because they can recognize and understand objects, gestures, and expressions. Visual literacy goes beyond simple perception and is a learned skill. One becomes visually literate by being able to identify the characteristics of images, to understand their functions, and to use visual images to communicate to others (Burmark, 2002). As the use of technology increases, it is important to be able to communicate effectively with digital, visual, and sound images. Educators need to do more than help students understand the isolated images, they need to help students develop the ability to think critically about the composition of the picture, enhancing their ability to read and analyze what they see (Burmark, 2002).

Teachers can use the following activities to promote their students' visual literacy:

1. Cut out photos from a newspaper or magazine. Look at the images, and make a list comparing the types of images and the techniques used in making them. How do words add to the images? What do the images relate about the people and places?

2. Choose a particular time period, and look at photos from that period in a photo gallery on the Internet. Write the story that the pictures tell.

3. Read the classified ads of a newspaper. Choose three apartments, cars, or other items that you are interested in. Make a chart comparing the features, prices, and incentives for each, and determine which is the best choice.

4. Draw a scene from a text. Describe the illustration.

5. Use maps, charts, tables, and graphs to enhance reading.

Gathering Data From Visual Representations

As noted earlier, newspapers and magazines are filled with visual representations such as maps, charts, tables, graphs, schedules, and even comics that students can study and analyze. For example, students can follow these visual representations over a period of time to study weather patterns, sports scores, election poll results, movie schedules, and even comic character representations, and students can record their information. Tama and McClain (2001) suggest that students might first construct a matrix to record the information they find and then choose an appropriate graphic representation, such as a bar graph, line graph, pie graph, table or chart, to report their findings and, finally, present a discussion of any trends that are present or any predictions they can make on the basis of the data they have discovered. This type of data collection engages students and helps them to understand the concepts they are being challenged to understand in the graphic representations they see. See Figure 6.16 for a sample matrix of data and Figure 6.17 for a graph and analysis of the matrix's information.

Results of Candidate Poll Across a One-Month Period

Date	Red Party Candidate	Blue Party Candidate
September 5	43%	57%
September 7	41%	59%
September 9	42%	58%
September 11	51%	49%
September 13	51%	49%
September 15	55%	45%
September 17	53%	47%
September 19	30%	70%
September 21	29%	71%
September 23	28%	72%
September 25	60%	40%
September 27	62%	38%
September 29	65%	35%
October 1	66%	34%

Figure 6.16   Example Matrix of Data Gathered From Visual Representations

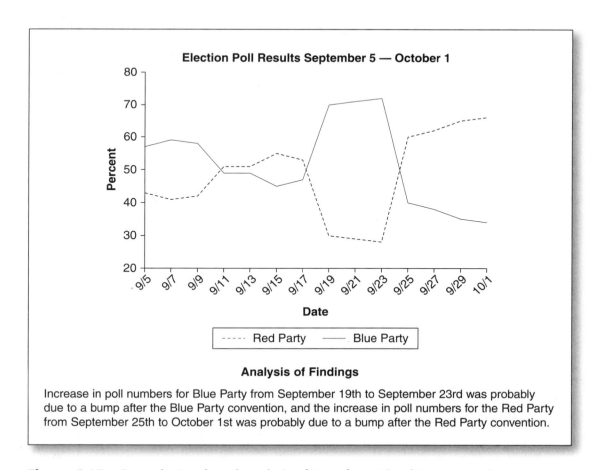

Analysis of Findings

Increase in poll numbers for Blue Party from September 19th to September 23rd was probably due to a bump after the Blue Party convention, and the increase in poll numbers for the Red Party from September 25th to October 1st was probably due to a bump after the Red Party convention.

Figure 6.17   Example Graph and Analysis of Data from Visual Representations

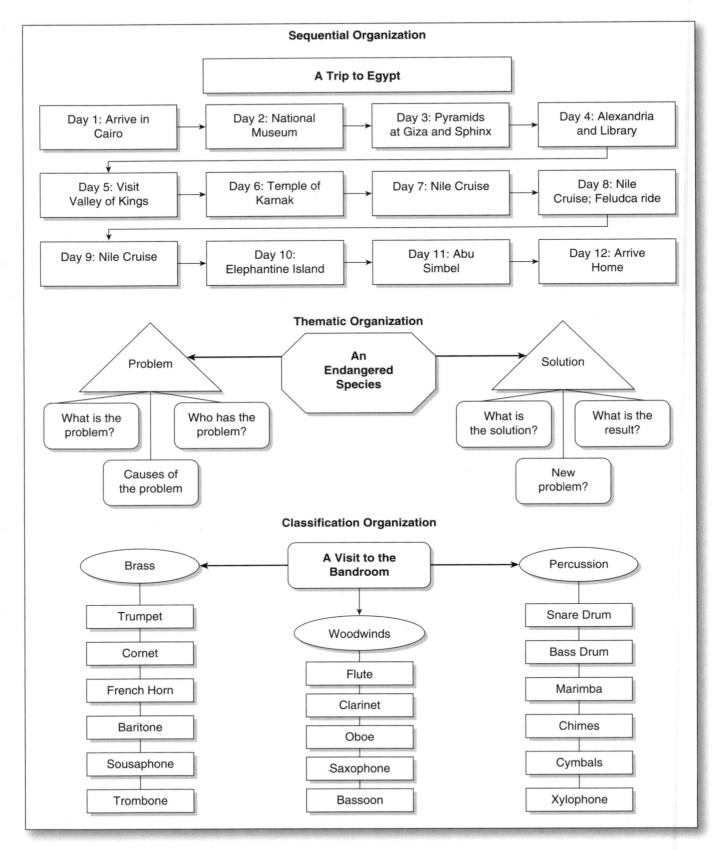

Figure 6.18   Storyboard Organizations Patterns

Storyboards

Storyboards, created by stringing a group of graphic organizers together, are most easily likened to a storybook, since they basically tell the story of each frame of a longer visual presentation. Since they contain all the components that will ultimately be in the final product, they are critical if the product needs to be edited or revised. A basic storyboard usually contains several segments or pages, each of which has a sketch of the needed graphic and the text to go with it, and a number to help in rearrangement and revision. The student's name and course or lesson information are also included.

Finally, according to Sinatra, Beaudry, Stahl-Gemake, and Guastello as reported in Roe et al. (2007), storyboards may be organized by sequence, theme, or classification. See Figure 6.18 for an example of storyboards for each of those organizational formats. Storyboards are used in digital storytelling as discussed above and in the strategies Photo Essays and You Ought to be in Pictures discussed below.

Photo Essays

Sinatra et al., as found in Roe et al. (2007), suggest that students, especially groups of students that are culturally diverse, benefit from using photographs to help them both organize their thinking and develop their writing skills.

Steps for Photo Essays

1. Students choose a topic and conduct research to locate facts about it.

2. Next, they collect pictures that relate to the topic and can be used to illustrate the facts they have found.

3. Once the pictures have been collected, students arrange them on a storyboard using one of the common storyboard organizational formats discussed above.

4. Finally, when the storyboard is complete, students write an essay on the topic.

You Ought to Be in Pictures

Buehl (2000) has created an effective strategy to help students relate to what they have read, especially as they read about events that are complex or that have happened in the past. This strategy asks students to process what they are asked to learn by using a sort of mental imagery. As Buehl (2001) points out, through the use of this strategy, students become personally engaged in their learning, since they make use of their imaginations as they study a topic rather than merely reading cold, impersonal text.

Steps for You Ought to Be in Pictures

1. Collect photographs that are related to the curriculum, unit, or lesson you are teaching.

2. Show students one of the photographs, and guide them through a mental imagery exercise by introducing the topic of the photo and then asking them to look closely at the picture and use all of their senses to imagine what the picture tells them about the topic you are teaching. They should especially focus on any people in the picture.

3. Next, ask the students to pretend either that they are in the picture or that they took the picture. Then ask them to imagine that they are showing this picture to someone else. What would they say? What memories do they have? How did they feel? What made them take the picture?

4. Finally, ask students to record these thoughts and feelings in a journal or an essay.

Using Television and Videos

Most classrooms now have televisions, which can be used for broadcasting daily announcements, previewing upcoming school events, and viewing educational programs and videos. If they are used effectively, films and videos can be powerful resources to reach learners with a broad range of skills. But, in order to promote effective learning, teachers should use the following three procedures when using television or video clips in the classroom:

1. **Previewing:** Determine what the students already know about the history, theory, or themes in the film. Make sure students are familiar with any new vocabulary.

2. **Viewing:** Make students accountable for the information provided in the film. You can prepare a handout with questions or a graph, or require the students to take notes.

3. **Postviewing:** Discuss the film, and conduct a follow up activity.

In addition, Tama and McClain (2001) suggest that viewing television, videos, or films provides an excellent opportunity for students to learn to detect bias as well as to differentiate fact from opinion. They detail an assignment developed by Becker (1973) that asks students to view a variety of talk shows, news reports, or documentaries and then determine how each covered a specific issue. Were all sides of the issue presented? Was a particular point of view stressed? Did the commentator, reporter, or host insert his or her opinion by using subjective or "loaded" words, specific facial expressions, vocal tones, or expressive gestures? Finally, students conclude their study by developing a matrix to compare their findings. Of course, students may work cooperatively by each viewing a separate program and then cooperatively comparing their findings. See Figure 6.19 for an example of this assignment and a matrix in which student responses are recorded.

Assignment: Listen to several local television and/or radio stations to hear their coverage of a news story of your choosing. Your task is to determine the following:

1. Did the stations give equal coverage to the story?

2. Did the stations give equal coverage to all sides of the issue?

3. Did the stations show any bias?

4. Did the stations present facts or opinions?

News Topic: Hurricane Kyle

ABC	*CBS*	*NBC*	*WGN*
• 5 minute coverage • Live feed on storm damage • Interview with mayor • "Loaded" words used: *devastating, life-threatening, never before seen*	• 3 minute coverage • Interview with townspeople • Interview with police chief • "Loaded" words used: *horrific*	• 1 minute coverage • Announcer report • Interview with weatherman • No "loaded" words used	• 30 second coverage • Comments made during weather forecast • No "loaded" words used

Figure 6.19   Example of TV Assignment

CHAPTER SUMMARY

In this age of technology, students are faced with a myriad of new literacies that provide them with a plethora of opportunities. And, these opportunities are changing what it means to be literate. This chapter discusses the new literacies that engage the students of today such as the Internet, informational literacy, media literacy, and visual literacy. In order to help students learn to use these new technological opportunities, this chapter provides a variety of learning strategies that can be used in all content areas.

References

Alejandro, A. (1989). Cars: A culturally integrated I Search module. *English Journal, 78*(1), 41–44.

Allen, C. A. (2001). *The multigenre research paper.* Portsmouth, NH: Heinemann.

Allen, J. (1999). *Words, words, words: Teaching vocabulary in grades 4–12.* York, ME: Stenhouse.

Allington, R. (2002). You can't learn much from books you can't read. *Educational Leadership, 60*(11), 37–43.

Allington, R. (2006). *What really matters for struggling readers: Designing research-based programs* (2nd ed.). Boston: Allyn & Bacon.

Alvermann, D. E. (1991). The discussion web: A graphic aid for learning across the curriculum. *The Reading Teacher, 45*(2), 92–99.

Alvermann, D. E., Dillon, D. R., & O'Brien, D. G. (1987). *Using discussion to promote reading comprehension.* Newark, DE: International Reading Association.

American Library Association Presidential Committee on Information Literacy. (1989). *Final report.* Chicago: American Library Association.

Armbruster, B., Anderson, T., Armstrong, J., Wise, M., Janisch, C., & Meyer, L. (1991). Reading and questioning in content areas. *Journal of Reading Behavior, 23*(1), 35–59.

Armbruster, B., Anderson, T. H., & Ostertag, J. (1989). Teaching text structure to improve reading and writing. *The Reading Teacher, 43*(2), 130–137.

Aronson, E., & Patnoe, S. (1997). *The jigsaw classroom: Building cooperation in the classroom* (2nd ed.). New York: Addison Wesley, Longman.

Association of College and Research Libraries (ACRL). (2000). *Information literacy competency standards for higher education.* Chicago: Author.

Ausubel, D. (1978). *Educational psychology: A cognitive view* (2nd ed.). New York: Holt, Rinehart, & Winston.

Bangert-Drowns, R. L., Hurley, M. M., & Wilkinson, B. (2004). The effects of school-based writing-to-learn interventions on academic achievement: A meta-analysis. *Review of Educational Research, 74*(1), 29–58.

Barr, M. A., & Healy, M. K. (1988). School and university articulation: Different contexts for writing across the curriculum. In S. H. McLeod (Ed.), *Strengthening programs for writing across the curriculum* (pp. 43–53). San Francisco, CA: Jossey-Bass. Retrieved November 5, 2004, from http://wac.colostate.edu/books/mcleod_programs/

Basurto, I. (2004). Teaching vocabulary creatively. In G. E. Tompkins & C. L. Blanchfield (Eds.), *Teaching vocabulary: 50 creative strategies, grades K–12* (pp. 1–4). Upper Saddle River, NJ: Pearson Education.

Beck, I. L., McKeown, M. G., Hamilton, R. L., & Kucan, L. (1997). *Questioning the author: An approach to enhancing student engagement with text.* Newark, DE: International Reading Association.

Beck, I. L., McKeown, M. G., & Kucan, L. (2002). *Bringing words to life: Robust vocabulary instruction.* New York: Guilford Press.

Becker, G. (1973). *Television and the classroom reading program.* Newark, DE: International Reading Association.

Biancarosa, G., & Snow, C. (2004). *Reading next—A vision for action and research in middle school and high school literacy: A report to the Carnegie Corporation of New York.* Washington, DC: Alliance for Excellent Education.

Biemiller, A. (2004). Teaching vocabulary in the primary grades: Vocabulary instruction needed. In J. F. Baumann & E. J. Kame'enui (Eds.), *Vocabulary instruction: From research to practice* (pp. 28–40). New York: Guilford Press.

Blachowicz, C., & Fisher, P. (2002). *Teaching vocabulary in all classrooms.* Upper Saddle River, NJ: Pearson Education.

Bleich, D. (1978). *Subjective criticism.* Baltimore: Johns Hopkins University Press.

Bloom, B. S. (1984). *Taxonomy of educational objectives, book I: Cognitive domain.* White Plains, NY: Longman.

Britton, J., Burgess, T., Martin, N., McLeod, A., & Rosen, H. (1975). *The development of writing abilities.* London: MacMillan.

Bruce, B. (2003). *Literacy in the information age: Inquiries into meaning making with new technologies.* Thousand Oaks, CA: Corwin.

Budiansky, S. (2001). The trouble with text books. *Prism, 10*(6), 24–27.

Buehl, D. (2000). You ought to be in pictures: Using photos to help students understand the past. *WEAC News and Views, 380*(18), 14.

Buehl, D. (2001). *Classroom strategies for interactive learning.* Newark, DE: International Reading Association.

Burke, J. (2000). *Reading reminders: Tools, tips, and techniques.* Portsmouth, NH: Boynton/Cook.

Burmark, L. (2002). *Visual literacy.* Alexandria, VA: Association for Supervision and Curriculum Development.

Busching, B. A., & Slesinger, B. A. (1995). Authentic questions: What do they look like? *Language Arts, 72*(5) 341–351.

Cantrell, R. J., Fusaro, J. A., & Dougherty, E. A. (2000). Exploring the effectiveness of journal writing on learning social studies: A comparative study. *Reading Psychology, 21*(1), 1–11.

Cazden, C. B. (1986). Classroom discourse. In M. Wittrock (Ed.), *Handbook of research on teaching* (3rd ed., pp. 432–462). New York: Macmillan.

Cazden, C. B. (1988). *Classroom discourse: The language of teaching and learning.* Portsmouth, NH: Heinemann.

Center for the Advancement of Teaching and Learning, Kansas State University. (2006). *Is discussion effective in the college classroom?* Retrieved September 23, 2009, from http://www.k-state.edu/catl/teach/gtahandbook/discuss.htm

Christenbury, L. (2006). *Making the journey: Being and becoming a teacher of English language arts.* Portsmouth, NH: Boynton/Cook.

Conley, M. (2008). *Content area literacy: Learners in context.* Boston: Pearson Education.

Considine, D. M., & Haley, G. E. (1999). *Visual messages: Integrating imagery into instruction* (2nd ed.). Englewood, CO: Teacher Ideas Press.

Cooter, R. B., Jr., & Chilcoat, G. W. (1991). Content focused melodrama: Dramatic renderings of historical text. *Journal of Reading, 34*(4), 274–277.

Coulter, B., Feldman, A., & Konold, C. (2000). Rethinking online adventures. *Learning and leading with technology, 28*(1), 42–47.

Cowan, G., & Cowan, E. (1980). *Writing.* New York: Wiley.

Crapse, L. (1995). Helping students construct meaning through their own questions. *Journal of Reading, 38*(5), 389–390.

Crawford, G. B. (2007). *Brain-based teaching with adolescent learning in mind.* Thousand Oaks, CA: Corwin.

Daniels, H. (2002). *Literature circles: Voice and choice in book clubs and reading groups.* Portland, ME: Stenhouse.

Denner, P. R., & McGinley, W. J. (1986). The effects of story-impressions as a prereading/writing activity on story comprehension. *Journal of Educational Research, 83*(6), 320–326.

Deschenes, C., Ebeling, D. G., & Sprague, J. (1994). *Adapting curriculum and instruction in inclusive classrooms: A teacher's desk reference.* Bloomington: Indiana University.

Dillon, J. T. (1988). *Questioning and teaching: A manual of practice.* New York: Teachers College Press.

Durkin, D. (1979). What classroom observations reveal about reading comprehension. *Reading Research Quarterly, 14*(4), 481–533.

Eanet, M., & Manzo, A. (1976). REAP—a strategy for improving reading/writing/study skills. *Journal of Reading, 8,* 647–652.

Emig, J. (1977). Writing as a mode of learning. *College Composition and Communication, 28*(2), 122–128.

Fisher, D., & Frey, D. (2008). *Improving adolescent literacy: Content area strategies at work.* Upper Saddle River, NJ: Pearson Education.

Fogarty, R. (1997). *Problem based learning and other curriculum models for the multiple intelligences classroom.* Thousand Oaks, CA: Corwin.

Fogarty, R. (2002). *The brain compatible classroom.* Thousand Oaks, CA: Corwin.

Forsman, S. (1985). Writing to learn means learning to think. In A. R. Gere (Ed.), *Roots in the sawdust: Writing to learn across the disciplines* (pp. 162–174). Urbana, IL: National Council of Teachers of English.

Fulwiler, T. (1982). Writing: An act of cognition. *New Directions for Teaching and Learning, 12,* 15–26.

Fulwiler, T. (Ed.). (1987). *The journal book.* Portsmouth, NH: Boynton/Cook.

Garber-Miller, K. (2007). Playful textbook previews: Letting go of familiar mustache monologues. *Journal of Adolescent and Adult Literacy, 50*(4), 284–288.

Gillet, J., & Kita, J. (1979). Words, kids, and categories. *Reading Teacher, 32*(5), 538–542.

Graves, M. F. (2000). A vocabulary program to complement and bolster a middle grade comprehension program. In B. M. Taylor, M. F. Graves, & P. Van Den Broek (Eds.), *Reading for meaning* (pp. 116–135). Newark, DE: International Reading Association & Teachers College Press.

Graves, M. F., & Watts-Taffe, S. M. (2002). The place of word-consciousness in a research-based vocabulary program. In A. E. Farstrup & S. J. Samuels (Eds.), *What research has to say about reading instruction* (3rd ed., pp. 140–165). Newark, DE: International Reading Association.

Greenwood, S. (2004). Content matters: Building vocabulary and conceptual understanding in the subject areas. *Middle School Journal, 35*(3), 27–34.

Grierson, S. T., Anson, A., & Baird, J. (2002). Exploring the past through multigenre writing. *Language Arts, 80*(1), 51–59.

Guthrie, J. T., & Davis, M. H. (2003). Motivating struggling readers in middle school through an engagement model of classroom practice. *Reading and writing quarterly, 19*(1), 59–85.

Harris, J. (1998). *Virtual architecture: Designing and directing curriculum based telecomputing.* Eugene, OR: International Society for Technology in Education.

Harste, J., Short, K., & Burke, C. (1988). *Creating classrooms for authors.* Portsmouth, NH: Heinemann.

Herber, H. (1978). *Teaching reading in content areas* (2nd ed.). Englewood Cliffs, NJ: Prentice-Hall.

Herrington, A. (1981). Writing to learn: Writing across the disciplines. *College English, 4*(4), 379–387.

Hickey, M. G. (1990). Reading and social studies: The critical connection. *Social Education, 54*(3), 175–179.

Hoffman, J. V. (1979). The intra-act procedure for critical reading. *Journal of Reading, 22*(7), 605–608.

Irvin, J. L. (1990). *Vocabulary knowledge: Guidelines for instruction.* Washington, DC: National Education Association.

Irvin, J. L., Buehl, D. R., & Radcliffe, B. J. (2007). *Strategies to enhance literacy and learning in middle school content area classrooms.* Boston: Pearson Education.

Ivey, G. (1999). A multicase study in the middle school: Complexities among young adolescent readers. *Reading Research Quarterly, 34*(2), 172–192.

Jensen, E. (2000). *Brain based learning.* San Diego, CA: The Brain Store.

Johns, J., & Berglund, R. (2002). *Strategies for content area learning.* Dubuque, IA: Kendall/Hunt.

Kintsch, W., & Van Dijk, T. (1978). Toward a model of text comprehension and production. *Psychological Review, 85*(5), 363–394.

Kist, W. (2005). *New literacies in action: Teaching and learning in multiple media.* New York: Teachers College Press.

Knoblauch, C. A., & Brannon, L. (1983). Writing as learning through the curriculum. *College English, 45*(5), 465–474.

Konopak, B. C., Martin, M. A., & Martin, S. H. (1987). Reading and writing: Aids to learning in the content areas. *Journal of Reading, 31*(2),109–115.

Langer, J. A., & Applebee, A. N. (2007). *How writing shapes thinking: A study of teaching and learning.* WAC Clearinghouse Landmark Publications in Writing Studies: http://wac.colostate.edu/books/langer_applebee/. Originally published in print, 1987, by National Council of Teachers of English, Urbana, IL.

Lee, J., Grigg, W., & Donahue, P. (2007). *The nation's report card: Reading 2007* (NCES 2007–496). Washington, DC: National Center for Education Statistics, Institute of Education Sciences, U.S. Department of Education.

Lenhart, A., Hitlin, P., & Madden, M. (2004, July 27). *Teens and technology.* Retrieved April 2, 2009 from Pew Internet & American Life Project, http://www.pewinternet.org

Lenters, K. (2006). Resistance, struggle, and the adolescent reader. *Journal of Adolescent and Adult Literacy, 50*(2), 136–148.

Leu, D. J. Jr., Kinzer, C. K., Coiro, J. L., & Cammack, D. W. (2004). Toward a theory of new literacies emerging from the Internet and other information and communication technologies. In R. B. Ruddell & N. J. Unrau (Eds.), *Theoretical models and practices of reading* (5th ed., pp. 1,570–1,613). Newark, DE: International Reading Association.

Leu, D. J. Jr., & Leu, D. D. (2000). *Teaching with the Internet: Lessons from the classroom* (3rd ed.). Norwood, MA: Christopher-Gordon.

Leu, D. J. Jr., Leu, D. D., & Coiro, J. L. (2006). *Teaching with the Internet K–12: New literacies for new times* (4th ed.). Norwood, MA: Christopher-Gordon.

Macrorie, K. (1988). *The I-search paper.* Portsmouth, NH: Heinemann.

Marzano, R. J. (2004). The developing vision of vocabulary instruction. In J. F. Baumann & E. J. Kame'enui (Eds.), *Vocabulary instruction: From research to practice* (pp. 159–176). New York: Guilford Press.

McGee, L. M. (1982). Awareness of text structure: Effects on children's recall of expository text. *Reading Research Quarterly, 17*(4), 581–590.

McGinley, W. J., & Denner, P. R. (1987). Story impressions: A pre-reading/writing activity. *Journal of Reading, 31*(3), 248–253.

Mehan, H. (1979). *Learning lessons.* Cambridge, MA: Harvard University Press.

Meyer, B. J. F., & Poon, L. W. (2001). Effects of structure strategy training and signaling on recall of text. *Journal of Educational Psychology, 93,* 141–159.

Mitchell, D. (1996). Writing to learn across the curriculum and the English teacher, *English Journal, 85*(5), 93–97.

Moore, D. W., & Moore, S. A. (1986). Possible sentences. In E. K. Dishner, T. W. Bean, J. E. Readence, & D. W. Moore (Eds.), *Reading in the content areas* (pp. 174–179). Dubuque, IA: Kendall/Hunt.

Moulton, M. R. (1999). The multigenre paper: Increasing interest, motivation and functionality in research. *Journal of Adolescent and Adult Literacy 42*(7), 528–539.

NAEP. (2005a, May 17). *Long-term trends: Reading performance level descriptions.* Retrieved September 19, 2008, from http://nces.ed.gov/nationsreportcard/ltt/readingdescriptions.asp

NAEP. (2005b, August 5). *Reading achievement by grade level performance.* Retrieved September 19, 2008, from http://nces.ed.gov/nationsreportcard/reading/achieveall.asp

Nagy, W. E. (1988). *Teaching vocabulary to improve reading comprehension.* Urbana, IL: National Council of Teachers of English, and Newark, DE: International Reading Association.

Nagy, W. E., Herman, P. A., & Anderson, R. C. (1985). Learning words from context. *Reading Research Quarterly, 20*(2), 233–253.

Nagy, W. E., & Scott, J. (2000). Vocabulary processes. In M. L. Kamil, P. B. Mosenthal, P. D. Pearson, & R. Barr (Eds.), *Handbook of reading research* (vol. 3, pp. 269–284). Mahwah, NJ: Erlbaum.

National Association for Media Literacy Education. (2008). *Definitions.* Retrieved September 30, 2009, from http://www.amlainfo.org/media-literacy/definitions

National Reading Panel. (2000). *Teaching children to read: An evidence-based assessment of the scientific research literature on reading and its implications for reading instruction* (National Institute of Health Pub. No. 00–4769). Washington, DC: National Institute of Child Health and Human Development.

Nelson, K. (2001). *Teaching in the cyberage: Linking the Internet and brain theory.* Thousand Oaks, CA: Corwin.

Newell, R. J. (2003). *Passion for learning: How project-based learning meets the needs of 21st-century students.* Lanham, MD: Scarecrow Press.

Niles, O. S. (1974). Organization perceived. In H. L. Herber (Ed.), *Perspectives in reading: Developing study skills in secondary schools* (pp. 77–97). Newark, DE: International Reading Association.

Odell, L. (1980). The process of writing and the process of learning. *College Composition and Communication, 31*(1), 42–50.

Parker, R. P. (1985). The language across the curriculum movement: A brief overview and bibliography. *College Composition and Communication, 36*(2), 173–177.

Pearson, P. D., & Gallagher, M. C. (1983). The instruction of reading comprehension. *Contemporary Educational Psychology, 8*(8), 317–344.

Peterson, C. L., Caverly, D. C., Nicholson, S. A., O'Neal, S., & Cusenbary, S. (2000). *Building reading proficiencies at the secondary level: A guide to resources.* Austin: Southwest Texas State University.

Potter, J. W. (2001). *Media literacy* (2nd ed.). London: Sage Publications.

Pressley, M. (2002). *Comprehension instruction: What makes sense now, what might make sense soon.* Retrieved November 8, 2005, from http://www.readingonline.org/articles/ art_index.asp?HREF=handbook/index.html

RAND Reading Study Group. (2002). *Reading for understanding: Toward an R&D program in reading comprehension.* Santa Monica, CA: RAND Corporation.

Raphael, T. E., Au, K. H., & Highfield, K. (2006). *QAR now.* New York: Scholastic.

Raphael, T. E., & Englert, C. S. (1990). Writing and reading: Partners in constructing meaning. *The Reading Teacher, 43*(6), 388–400.

Readence, J. E., Bean, T. W., & Baldwin, R. S. (2004). *Content area literacy: An integrated approach.* Dubuque, IA: Kendall/Hunt.

Reeves, A. R. (2004). *Adolescents talk about reading: Exploring resistance to and engagement with text.* Newark, DE: International Reading Association.

Rhoder, C. (2002). Mindful reading: Strategy training that facilitates transfer. *Journal of Adolescent and Adult Literacy, 45*(6), 498–512.

Richardson, J. S., & Morgan, R. F. (2003). *Reading to learn in the content areas.* Belmont, CA: Wadsworth.

Roblyer, M. D. (2003). *Integrating educational technology into teaching.* Columbus, OH: Merrill/Prentice-Hall.

Roe, B. D., Stoodt-Hill, B. D., & Burns, P. (2007). *Secondary school literacy instruction: The content areas.* Boston: Houghton Mifflin.

Rogers, T. (1990). A point counterpoint response strategy for complex short stories. *The Journal of Reading, 34*(4), 278–282.

Romano, T. (2000). *Blending genre: Altering style.* Portsmouth, NH: Boynton/Cook.

Rosenblatt, L. M. (1938). *Literature as exploration.* New York: D. Appleton–Century.

Rosenblatt, L. M. (1994). *The reader, the text, the poem: The transactional theory of the literary work.* Carbondale: Southern Illinois University Press.

Ruddell, R. B. (2006). *Teaching children to read and write: Becoming an effective literacy teacher.* Boston: Pearson Education.

Ryder, R. J., & Graves, M. F. (1994). *Reading and learning in content areas.* Columbus, OH: Merrill.

Sagoff, M. (1971). *Shrinklits.* New York: Doubleday.

Samuels, S. J. (2002). Reading fluency: Its development and assessment. In A. E. Farstrup & S. J. Samuels (Eds.), *What research has to say about reading instruction* (3rd ed., pp. 166–183). Newark, DE: International Reading Association.

Santa, C. M. (1988). *Content reading including study systems.* Dubuque, IA: Kendall/Hunt.

Santa, C. M. (2006). A vision for adolescent literacy: Ours or theirs? *Journal of Adolescent and Adult Literacy, 49*(8), 486–476.

Schwartz, R., & Raphael, T. (1985). Concept of definition: A key to improving students' vocabulary. *The Reading Teacher, 39*(2), 198–205.

Scott, J. A., & Nagy, W. E. (1997). Understanding the definitions of unfamiliar words. *Reading Research Quarterly, 32*(2), 184–200.

Seven steps to create a DigiTales story. (2004). Retrieved September 28, 2009, from http://www.digitales.us/resources/seven_steps.php#

Shanahan, T. (Ed.). (1990). *Reading and writing together: New perspectives for the classroom.* Norwood, MA: Christopher-Gordon.

Sharrer, E. (2003). Making a case for media literacy in the curriculum: Outcomes and assessment. *Journal of Adolescent and Adult Literacy, 48*(4), 354–358.

Shu, H., Anderson, R., & Zhang, H. (1995). Incidental learning of word meanings while reading: A Chinese and American cross-cultural study. *Reading Research Quarterly, 30*(1), 76–95.

Silver, H. F., Strong, R. W., & Perini, M. J. (2001). *Tools for promoting active, in-depth learning.* Ho-Ho-Kus, NJ: Thoughtful Education Press.

Silver, H. F., Strong, R. W., & Perini, M. J. (2007). *The strategic teacher: Selecting the right research-based strategy for every lesson.* Alexandria, VA: Association for Supervision and Curriculum Development.

Sizer, T. R. (1984). *Horace's compromise: The dilemma of the American high school.* Boston: Houghton Mifflin.

Smith, P., & Tompkins, G. (1988). Structured notetaking: A new strategy for content areas. *Journal of Reading, 32*(1), 46–53.

Smith, S., & Bean, R. (1980). The guided writing procedure: Integrating content reading and writing improvement. *Reading World, 19*(3), 290–294.

Stahl, S. A., & Fairbanks, M. M. (1986). The effects of vocabulary instruction: A model based meta analysis. *Review of Educational Research, 56*(1), 72–110.

Stepien, W. J., and Gallagher, S. A. (1993). Problem based learning: As authentic as it gets. *Educational Leadership, 50*(7), 25–28.

Tama, M. C., & McClain, A. B. (2001). *Guiding reading and writing in the content areas: Practical strategies.* Dubuque, IA: Kendall/Hunt.

Taylor, B. M., & Samuels, S. J. (1983). Children's use of text structure in the recall of expository material. *American Educational Research Journal, 20*(4), 517–528.

Tierney, R. J., & Pearson, P. D. (1983). Toward a composing model of reading. *Language Arts, 60*(5), 568–580.

Tierney, R. J., & Readence, J. E. (2005). *Reading strategies and practices: A compendium* (6th ed.). Boston: Pearson Education.

Tomlinson, S. (1990). Writing to learn: Back to another basic. *New Directions for Teaching and Learning, 1990*(42), 31–39.

Unrau, N. (2008). *Content area reading and writing: Fostering literacies in middle and high school cultures.* Upper Saddle River, NJ: Pearson Education.

Vacca, R. T., & Vacca, J. L. (2008). *Content area reading: Literacy and learning across the curriculum.* Boston: Pearson Education.

Vaughn, C. L. (1990). Knitting writing: The double-entry journal. In N. Atwell (Ed.), *Coming to know: Writing to learn in intermediate grades* (pp. 69–75). Portsmouth, NH: Heinemann.

WestEd. (2002). *Key ideas of the strategic literacy initiative.* Retrieved September 29, 2009, from http://www.wested.org/stratlit/about/keyideas.shtml

Wiggins, G., & McTighe, J. (2005). *Understanding by design* (2nd ed.). Alexandria, VA: Association for Supervision and Curriculum Development.

Winograd, P., & Hare, V. C. (1988). Direct instruction of reading comprehension strategies: The nature of teacher explanation. In C. E. Weinstein, E. T. Goetz, & P. A. Alexander (Eds.), *Learning and study strategies: Issues in assessment, instruction and evaluation* (pp. 121–139). San Diego, CA: Academic Press.

Wood, K. D. (1984). Probable passages: A writing strategy. *The Reading Teacher, 37*(5), 496–499.

Wood, K. D. (1988). Guiding students through informational text. *The Reading Teacher, 41*(9), 912–920.

Wood, K. D., Lapp, D., & Flood, J. (1992). *Guiding readers through text: A review of study guides.* Newark, DE: International Reading Association.

Woodward, A., & Elliott, D. L. (1990). Textbooks: Consensus and controversy. In D. L. Elliott & A. Woodward (Eds.), *Textbooks and schooling in the United States* (Eighty-ninth yearbook of the National Society for the Study of Education, Part I, pp. 146–161). Chicago: University of Chicago Press.

Index

CORWIN

A SAGE Company

The Corwin logo—a raven striding across an open book—represents the union of courage and learning. Corwin is committed to improving education for all learners by publishing books and other professional development resources for those serving the field of PreK–12 education. By providing practical, hands-on materials, Corwin continues to carry out the promise of its motto: **"Helping Educators Do Their Work Better."**